pure chocolate

❧{ pure chocolate }❧

Divine Desserts and Sweets from
the Creator of Fran's Chocolates

FRAN BIGELOW with Helene Siegel

Broadway Books
New York

BROADWAY

PRINTED IN JAPAN

BROADWAY BOOKS and its logo, a letter B bisected on the diagonal, are trademarks of Random House, Inc.

Visit our website at www.broadwaybooks.com

First edition published 2004

BOOK DESIGN BY *Vertigo Design*, NYC
PHOTOGRAPHY BY Sang An
FOOD STYLIST: Jee Levin
PROP STYLIST: Phillippa Brathwaite
ILLUSTRATED BY *John Burgoyne*

Library of Congress Cataloging-in-Publication Data
Bigelow, Fran, 1943–
    Pure chocolate / Fran Bigelow with Helene Siegel.
        p. cm.
    Includes index.
    ISBN 0-7679-1658-1
        1. Cookery (Chocolate) 2. Chocolate desserts. I. Siegel, Helene. II. Title.
TX767.C5B49 2004
641.6'374—dc22

2003063591

10   9   8   7   6   5   4   3

{ to peter, dylan, and andrina }

ACKNOWLEDGMENTS

pure chocolate is an outgrowth of twenty years at Fran's Chocolates, and many of the people who helped with the book were there nearly from the beginning.

Kim Smith, one of the original pastry chefs from the shop, has been an invaluable help. She gave me the encouragement to write the book in the first place, and then was instrumental in translating the recipes from the early years at Fran's into easy-to-execute desserts for the home baker. Kim also brought her inimitable hands and eyes to making many of the desserts for the photo sessions. Her steady support and good humor have been priceless.

I have always been fortunate at Fran's in having the most wonderful, hardworking, and talented staff. Without them this book would not have been possible. Special thanks to Sean Seedlock and Dylan Bigelow for their leadership, dedication, and talent. They allowed me to concentrate on the book without worry.

To Sean, for his many years of dedication, his impeccable taste, and valuable suggestions. And to my son, Dylan, for his depth of knowledge, his passion, and his drive to continue to push the boundaries of fine chocolate. His suggestions on and critique of the manuscript were always helpful. He is a major source of inspiration in my work.

At home, thanks to Andrina, my daughter, for her infectious optimism and encouragement. She is wise beyond her years.

{ to peter, dylan, and andrina }

ACKNOWLEDGMENTS

pure chocolate is an outgrowth of twenty years at Fran's Chocolates, and many of the people who helped with the book were there nearly from the beginning.

Kim Smith, one of the original pastry chefs from the shop, has been an invaluable help. She gave me the encouragement to write the book in the first place, and then was instrumental in translating the recipes from the early years at Fran's into easy-to-execute desserts for the home baker. Kim also brought her inimitable hands and eyes to making many of the desserts for the photo sessions. Her steady support and good humor have been priceless.

I have always been fortunate at Fran's in having the most wonderful, hardworking, and talented staff. Without them this book would not have been possible. Special thanks to Sean Seedlock and Dylan Bigelow for their leadership, dedication, and talent. They allowed me to concentrate on the book without worry.

To Sean, for his many years of dedication, his impeccable taste, and valuable suggestions. And to my son, Dylan, for his depth of knowledge, his passion, and his drive to continue to push the boundaries of fine chocolate. His suggestions on and critique of the manuscript were always helpful. He is a major source of inspiration in my work.

At home, thanks to Andrina, my daughter, for her infectious optimism and encouragement. She is wise beyond her years.

To Peter, my husband, number-one supporter, cheerleader, and adviser. When the going gets tough, he is always there to pull me through.

In Seattle, Tom Douglas gets thanks for introducing me to his agent, Judith Riven. Judith was key to turning a dream into a reality and guiding me, a newcomer, on the somewhat complicated path to publication. She deserves an award for perseverance, good judgment, and introducing me to the writer Helene Siegel.

In New York, we want to thank the dedicated team at Broadway Books for giving us such a beautiful book. Thanks to Jennifer Josephy, our editor, who believed in the idea, supported it, and became our champion—and her assistant, Allyson Giard. Thanks to Umi Kenyon, art director, for her clear vision. Umi put together the most extraordinary team of Sang An, photographer, Jee Levin, food stylist, and Phillippa Braithwaite, prop stylist. These talented artists have brought all of our most delirious chocolate dreams to mouthwatering life.

Helene would also like to thank her family, Ted, Joe, and Andrew, for always being there—through good chocolate and bad. And a big thanks to Peter Barrett, her computer guru and friend.

∗{ fran bigelow }∗

{ contents }

❧{ introduction }❧

MAKING OF A CHOCOLATIER

A few lucky people are born to chocolate. Others, like myself, fall into it later in life and spend the rest of their lives mastering its magic. This is the story of how I found my passion and turned it into a thriving small business working with the world's most sublime ingredient.

When I graduated in 1964 with a degree in business from the University of Washington, the career outlook for women was cloudy at best. Women were a distinct minority in the business school, and finding a job after graduation was not a foregone conclusion.

The two jobs I held while my husband, Peter, attended graduate school—assistant at a brokerage house and cost accountant at a gas company—did not thrill me. By the time our son, Dylan, was born and Peter landed his first job, as a hospital administrator, I was more than willing to take a break and raise my children. After all, my mother, Marguerite, had been quite content as a stay-at-home mother and fabulous hostess.

Peter's job meant relocating to Berkeley, an exciting place to be in the early seventies. While the Berkeley campus was a hotbed of student activism, a small community of artisan bakers, chefs, and restaurateurs like Alice Waters were laying the groundwork for the new American cuisine that flowered in the eighties. During those heady days in Berkeley, while home raising our two children—Dylan was followed by our daughter, Andrina, four years later—I began cooking.

Like many women of my day, I had not cooked in my mother's kitchen. I started learning by working my way through Julia Child's cookbooks, mastering puff pastry, cutting up a chicken for coq au vin, and letting my egg dough rise slowly for the family's morning brioches. When it came to pastry, I was always tireless, keeping a steady stream of cakes, tarts, and cookies in the house at all times. One thing about the Bigelow household then and now—we never skip dessert.

As part of my explorations, I threw myself into entertaining family and friends with elaborate made-from-scratch dinner parties. When I realized that I wanted to go further with my cooking, I found the teacher who was to become my inspiration.

Josephine Araldo, a 1921 graduate of the Cordon Bleu in Paris, had a zest for life that was contagious. After cooking for Premier Georges Clemençeau and dancer Isadora Duncan in France, she moved to the States to be personal chef to a prominent San Francisco family. In retirement, Araldo gathered small groups in her apartment near Golden Gate Park for lessons in cooking and in life. She embodied the spirit of the resourceful French housewife, counseling her students to start a herb garden and passing along wisdom like "sending a man to the store is like sending no one"—ideas that resonated in those early days of fresh food and feminism. Any mistake in the kitchen could be fixed with a degree of ingenuity, Josephine assured us—except for pastry, which she avoided since it demanded complete perfection. Candy making was definitely also not her forte. Each class ended with the group sharing a lively meal at Josephine's well-set table while her husband, Charles, serenaded the group on his accordion. Josephine was eighty-two years old at the time.

This lively Frenchwoman opened a window into a life filled with the pleasure of finding work you love. It sparked something in me that hadn't been touched before. And so I started taking myself and my cooking more seriously. Aware that my penchant for detail and precision could find natural expression in the pastry kitchen, I enrolled in the pastry program at the California Culinary Academy across the bridge in San Francisco.

I studied with European pastry chefs and learned the skills and discipline required in baking. I also realized I wanted to bring the same standards for pure flavor and natural ingredients to desserts as was then being brought to the rest of the meal by people like Alice Waters in Berkeley.

The idea for my first shop may have been kindled in Berkeley, but I had to return to Seattle to bring it to fruition. By the time Peter and I moved back to Seattle, I was thirty-eight years old and had spent five years dreaming of my own business. By then I knew that

memories of mounds

When people ask me about the roots of my passion for chocolate, I have to return to childhood memories. Candy loomed large in my childhood, as it does for most folks. In 1940s and 1950s Seattle there were some great candy shops where quality and hand-craftsmanship were prized. Luckily for me, my grandmother Frances Hazel, a woman of exacting standards, wasn't above seeking out each one of them. I believe she visited every chocolate shop between Vancouver and Seattle to leave no chocolate box top unturned. I adored accompanying her on her tasting expeditions.

Downtown Seattle housed two shrines to sweets in my young eyes: Horluck's for sublime ice cream sundaes that were always too large to finish, and Frederick & Nelson's department store for their Victorian creams and personalized Easter eggs—a Seattle tradition I continue in my shops.

Left to my own devices, however, the Mounds bar was my obsession. Then as now, price was never a consideration in the serious pursuit of good candy. My family still chuckles about my determination when, on a daily allowance of a nickel a day during our summers on Camano Island, I would wait two days to save a dime for my beloved chocolate-covered coconut bar rather than settle for something less sublime.

Many years later, when the Mounds bar lost its allure for me, I created the Coconut Gold Bar—an homage to Mounds and my grandmother. It's covered with dark Belgian chocolate, topped with toasted almonds, and filled with a luscious white chocolate–coconut filling reminiscent of grandma Hazel's wonderful vanilla cream pudding.

if I wanted a meaningful life, it would have to include work. With both kids in school and the pastries piling up in the kitchen Peter finally gave me the push I needed. Tired of listening to my daydreams, he staked me to the first pastry shop with the admonition, "You won't be happy unless you try it."

When I opened my first shop, Fran's Patisserie and Chocolate Specialties on Madison Street, I thought small. I figured if I could sell ten cakes a day, pay my part-time baker and full-time salesperson, and remain in business, I was doing well. My goal was to re-create what I had experienced in the pastry and chocolate shops of France on my first trip to Europe in 1969—those perfect moments of bliss that only the finest desserts and chocolate can provide. Infused with the idealism of those early days in Berkeley, I was on a mission to change the world—or at least Seattle—one cake at a time. I vowed never to compromise on quality or flavor—a principle that still guides me today.

Back in pre-tech Seattle my idea of a chocolate salon may have been a stretch, but I was optimistic. After all, Americans were beginning to travel more, the food revolution was in full swing, and I was convinced that there was a small group of people who were willing to seek out the best in food. Artisan cheesemakers were making goat cheese in Sonoma, small farmers were growing fresh herbs, and extra-virgin olive oil had more buzz than a Hollywood starlet. My loyal customers at the beginning were people who had experienced chocolates at the best shops in Paris and were thrilled to find something comparable in their own backyard. One customer would send his chauffeur with an ice chest to pick up his weekly supply of truffles.

My whole family pitched in at the beginning. My father, who had been a small business owner himself, advised on major equipment installations. Peter did deliveries to restaurants on Saturdays, the kids worked behind the counter in the summer, and even my perfectly manicured mother, Marguerite, enjoyed chatting up the customers as she handed out samples from her silver tray.

What started as a pastry shop with one tray of dark chocolate truffles on the counter gradually evolved into a chocolate shop. As word spread about the truffles, I witnessed the irresistible power of pure chocolate. I saw one young man bring each new girlfriend to the shop to gauge her responses to our sensual chocolates; I saw children's faces light up when they received a perfect Easter egg with their names inscribed in white chocolate; and I was inspired by the elderly couple who visited the shop once a week to purchase eight chocolate truffles—one to share each day and one each for Sunday. To this day I still love to watch people's joy when they take their first bite of a pure chocolate truffle or cake.

That community connection is especially strong during the holiday season. As a little girl who lived for the holidays, I adored playing a part in so many people's celebrations. There was nothing more magical than my mother's home at Christmas, and at the chocolate shops I try to carry that tradition forward. Whether it's supplying a Seattle family's traditional bûche de Noël for ten years, personalizing Easter eggs for my early clients' children and grandchildren, or selecting hand-dipped and decorated truffles to spell out "I love you" for my own children on Valentine's Day, the responsibility of making everyone's special moments stellar is one I always take to heart.

ABOUT THE RECIPES

If I have learned one thing after twenty years in the chocolate kitchen, it is that if you don't respect chocolate's special characteristics, it is bound to cause you trouble. However, if you are patient and understand its unique properties, chocolate will repay you with the most perfect pleasure. Each time I walk into my kitchen, I continue to be amazed at chocolate's ability to teach me something new.

The recipes you are about to try represent the best from twenty-plus years of serious dessert making and tasting. Some, like L'Orange (page 52) and Tropicale (page 126), are old favorites from the original pastry shop. Others, like the Chocolate Cabernet Torte (page 73) and Ginger Key Lime Ice Cream (page 148) are more recent creations.

Many recipes, like the Chocolate Wafers (page 39), are exactly the same formulations as those sold in the shops and catalog. A few treats represent easier versions of favorites that were once sold at the shop, like the Gold Bar Brownies (page 34). If you have ever yearned for the Chocolate Espresso Torte (page 71), Chocolate-Stuffed Figs (page 210), or Deepest, Darkest Chocolate Sauce (page 172) but couldn't wait for the delivery truck to arrive, now you can have the satisfaction of making your own perfect desserts at home in just a few short hours.

Many of these chocolate desserts have been cooked thousands of times for my shops. All of them have been tested in small batches in my home kitchen to meet my finicky standards for inclusion in the book. All of the tips for success that you need have been included in the recipes. All you need to do is follow the directions and I can guarantee you a sublime dessert every time.

To get off to the best possible start, please absorb these ground rules first:

- Read the recipes *carefully*, all the way through, before putting together your shopping list. Do not forget finishes and glazes when shopping.

- Baking is not rocket science, but it is a kind of science, so you want to follow these instructions *exactly*. If the recipe is several parts, be sure to read all the parts and prepare them in the proper sequence.

- Always purchase the finest chocolate you can afford, preferably following the recommendations in the recipe. You would be amazed at the different results the same recipe can yield with different chocolates. High-quality chocolate will immediately elevate your chocolate desserts to a more intense level. Over the last ten years there has been an explosion in the availability of fine chocolate in this country, which means that supermarkets now carry excellent chocolate.

- Great chocolate desserts are the result of precise attention to detail. When you read the recipes, pay close attention to timing and temperature, and follow them to the letter. These crucial factors will make all the difference in the final product.

- In baking pans, size really matters. Use only the size pan specified, or all of your efforts may go to waste.

- Do not be concerned if your finished chocolate desserts—especially the tortes and cakes—seem too small to make the number of servings in the recipe. Trust me. These flavors and textures are so intense that for most people a small sliver will satisfy even the most insatiable chocolate lover. If you have already developed a taste for very fine chocolate desserts, you know that a little bit goes a long way.

- Unless otherwise noted, all recipes should be served at room temperature, to bring out the full flavor of the chocolate. Allow 30 minutes to 1 hour to bring refrigerated desserts to room temperature.

{ travels with chocolate }

*i*n 1993 my husband, Peter, and I traveled to France for research purposes. I came back inspired. I wanted to duplicate in Seattle that sublime first spoonful of Paris's Berthillon ice cream. At that tiny shrine to ice cream on Ile St. Louis, I experienced flavors so saturated that they remain signposts I continue to strive for in all of my confections.

The fine craftsmanship and generosity of the Bernachon family of Lyon also left a lasting impression. Maurice Bernachon, the patriarch of this small family business, gave us a private tour of their facilities, where I was able to witness how a master chocolatier can control the whole process from selecting and roasting the beans to the jewel-like truffles sold in the shop. Bernachon was one of the few chocolatiers who insisted on making his own chocolate from scratch. The gorgeous wood paneling and solemnity of the almost 200-year-old Debauve et Gallais store, the oldest maker of handmade chocolate in Paris, fueled my dreams of beautiful chocolate salons where people could indulge in a complete sensory experience while selecting their chocolates.

That research trip was two weeks of pure heaven. With a guidebook by the renowned chocolate club that rates every noteworthy pastry shop and chocolatier—*Le Guide des Croquers de Chocolat*—tucked under our arms, we traveled all over France and tasted at about two shops a day. In addition to the influences I've already mentioned, the most lasting memories are of Robert Linxe's extraordinary Maison du Chocolat in Paris; Puyricard's brandied prune encased in chocolate in Aix; and the exquisite Wittamer in Brussels, my favorite pastry shop in the world.

Where to begin? The more experienced dessert maker will have no trouble jumping in almost anywhere and having great success. Most of my recipes are based on very few ingredients and rely on a small battery of equipment. As a purist, I strive to bring out the true flavor of chocolate and let the chocolate be the hero. I like to pare away flavors that might distract from chocolate, including sugar. My goal in these recipes is to preserve the pure, clean flavor of chocolate and bring out its depth and complexity by building layers of flavor that heighten the experience. This collection focuses on the classic complementary combinations such as coffee, raspberry, coconut, and orange.

I recommend that less experienced dessert makers begin with the baking recipes. There are fewer variables once the batter is mixed and placed in the oven than there are in a recipe cooked on the stovetop.

I would be remiss not to point out a few of the easiest, most delicious recipes in the book for those of you who want a quick chocolate hit.

- Turn straight to the Pure Chocolate Tart (page 79). And L'Orange (page 52) and Pavé Josephine (page 69) in the torte chapter.

- The Chocolate Wafers (page 39) and Chocolate Madeleines (page 48) in the cookies chapter

- The exquisite Pure Chocolate (page 170) and Chocolate Espresso sauces (page 171), which take only moments to make

- Chocolate Pots de Crème (page 142), as foolproof a pudding as you'll find

- Any of the beverages (see page 179) is a quick and easy route to a daily dose of chocolate.

But why rush it? My twenty years of experimentation and innovation should guide you to spectacular results each time. I hope you will savor each step in the process and each lovely bite just as much as I have enjoyed letting you in on my secrets.

All chocolate is made from the fruit of the cacao tree, which thrives in the tropical regions twenty degrees north and south of the equator. Scientists believe that the first cacao tree was found in the lower Amazon Basin in Venezuela. Twice a year the hard, squashlike pods are hand harvested and carefully split open to remove the beans (which are then allowed to naturally ferment and air-dry for several days).

Dried beans are sold to brokers, who in turn supply the chocolate manufacturers of the world. Most cacao beans are shipped to Europe and North America to be made into chocolate in a complex process that begins with cleaning and roasting and ends with molding liquid chocolate into bars.

It is the selection of the beans and their blending that most determines the quality of the finished product. Only a small percentage of the beans being harvested today are criollos, a premium flavor bean. Most chocolate is made from a blend of forasteros, a hardy bulk bean. Only the premium manufacturers are seeking out and paying the price for the rare criollos and the hybrid trinitarios, a bean that combines the robustness of forastero with the flavor of criollo.

After the beans are roasted according to each maker's style, they go through a grinding process that creates cocoa mass. The mass is then combined with cocoa butter, sugar, and vanilla for flavor accents, conched for smoothness, tempered for longevity, and molded into large bulk chocolate bars that are then wrapped and shipped. A chocolatier such as Fran's purchases the chocolate at this stage.

CHOOSING CHOCOLATE FOR DESSERT MAKING

It can't be overstressed that the quality of the chocolate used is what can elevate a bite of cake or a sip of hot chocolate into a life-altering moment. No matter how good your technique, if you are using inferior chocolate your dessert simply won't be as ravishing. The manufacturers I rely on for my chocolate are Callebaut, Valrhona, El Rey, Michel Cluizel, and Scharffen Berger. They all sell bars at supermarkets, specialty shops, by mail order, and on websites (see page 227).

Before you choose, it's important to know how to read a label. Be sure you are purchasing pure chocolate that contains only chocolate (beans, mass, or liquor), sugar, cocoa butter, vanilla, and lecithin. No vegetable fats should be listed as an ingredient.

Cacao percentage indicates the amount of cacao in relation to sugar. Thus a bar containing 60 percent cacao has 40 percent sugar, with less than one-half percent vanilla or lecithin. Of that 60 percent cacao, about half is cocoa solids and the other half is cocoa butter—for that marvelous melt-in-your-mouth consistency. All you need to remember is that the higher the percentage of cacao, the deeper, darker, and more pronounced the chocolate flavor. Another way to think of it is that if the cacao percentage dips below 50 percent, that chocolate bar contains more sugar than cacao, meaning less chocolate flavor—a sacrilege as far as I'm concerned. For these recipes, I do not recommend any dark chocolate where sugar is listed as the first ingredient.

The recipes in this book mostly call for dark, semisweet, or bittersweet chocolate, with some high-quality milk chocolate, white chocolate, and unsweetened chocolate. Where I felt it made a difference, I recommended an exact percentage of cacao or a specific maker. These recommendations are not meant to send you off in search of the holy grail. As long as your chocolate is from one of the better makers and within the general range of cacao content, your *Pure Chocolate* desserts should all be spectacular. Another philosophy to keep in mind when selecting a chocolate for a dessert is to choose one you would enjoy eating by itself. This is where your chocolate-tasting experience will serve you well.

Just as each coffee roaster has a style, each chocolate manufacturer develops a flavor and texture profile. To my mind, the Belgians make a chocolate with a subtle roast and round pleasing flavor—such as Callebaut. The French, on the other hand, like their chocolate the way they do their coffee, with a darker roast and stronger flavor—such as Valrhona. El Rey, from Venezuela with its flavorful beans, also has an assertive style. Scharffen Berger, the premium American manufacturer, is relatively new to the field. This company has developed a style all its own and is making intensely flavored chocolate.

Preferences in chocolate are extremely personal. Taste, reflect, and experiment—consider it the icing on the cake in your chocolate education.

Here are my current favorites by category to help you make your own selections for dessert making. It can be confusing because in the United States 35 percent cocoa mass is the only requirement for calling a chocolate either bittersweet or semisweet. Ten percent is the legal minimum cacao content for milk chocolate. Below are the guidelines that I follow in *Pure Chocolate* and all my recipes. The chocolate world is expanding rapidly as Americans' tastes change, so keep on checking the shelves—and tasting, of course.

semisweet

52 to 62 percent cacao: Semisweet chocolate is entry level for those who are new to darker, more pronounced chocolate flavor. Callebaut's 56 percent is my kitchen workhorse. With its accessible flavor and creamy consistency, it is a dream to work with. It melts easily, combines well with other flavors, and is fantastic for dipping. Other chocolates to use are: Cluizel, Valrhona, Scharffen Berger, El Rey, and Lindt, all available at supermarkets.

bittersweet

63 to 72 percent cacao: Darker and more pronounced in flavor than a semisweet, bittersweets are the favorites of many chefs. However, their higher cacao content can make them trickier to work with. For top-notch chocolate flavor in a bittersweet I enjoy: Valrhona, Callebaut, Scharffen Berger, Lindt, E. Guittard, Cluizel, and El Rey.

milk chocolate

36 to 46 percent cacao: As a rule, look for the darkest milk chocolate you can find for these recipes. The pronounced caramel flavor from the milk is delicious. The premium milk chocolates from Cluizel, El Rey, Valrhona, Callebaut, E. Guittard, and Lindt are all excellent.

white chocolate

Since it does not contain cacao solids, white chocolate is technically not a chocolate. Whether or not you're a fan of this bar of cocoa butter, sugar, vanilla, and milk, there are times when it is just right. I love it in whipped cream, and it is the perfect sweet counterpoint in a sophisticated cake like the bittersweet Blanc et Noir (page 101). White chocolate is very easy to work with. Just make sure you choose one with no added vegetable fat. El Rey, Valrhona, Lindt, and Callebaut make excellent white-chocolate bars.

unsweetened chocolate

100 percent cacao: Unsweetened chocolate, as the name implies, is 100 percent cacao with no sugar added. One taste will tell you that it is not meant to be eaten alone. I like to use it in combination with semi- or bittersweet to add depth of flavor. You can also improvise a bittersweet by substituting about 20 percent unsweetened chocolate and 80 percent semisweet for the quantity of bittersweet specified in the recipe. Valrhona and Scharffen Berger make excellent unsweetened bars.

cocoa powder

The recipes in the book all call for Dutch-processed cocoa—totally unsweetened cocoa whose natural acidity has been neutralized by an alkali. Dutch-processed cocoa gives darker chocolate results than ordinary unsweetened cocoa. Cocoa lends chocolate wafers, ice cream, and sorbets wonderful depth of flavor. I prefer Valrhona or Droste cocoa powder.

WORKING WITH PURE CHOCOLATE

melting chocolate

A sensitive moment in any chocolate recipe occurs at the beginning, when the chocolate is melted. Few things in the kitchen are more depressing and beyond repair than coarse, grainy, scorched chocolate. Just keep in mind that chocolate's two archenemies are heat and moisture. If you always melt over gentlest heat and are vigilant about stray drops of water, there shouldn't be a problem. After a little practice you'll wonder what all the fuss was about.

It doesn't take any fancy equipment to melt chocolate. I improvise a double boiler by choosing a stainless-steel bowl that can nestle on top of a small saucepan. Fill the pan with about 1 inch of water and bring to a simmer over lowest heat. Chop the chocolate into small-size pieces and place in the bowl over, but not touching, the water in the pan. Let sit, without stirring, until about half melted. Then remove from the heat, placing the bowl's bottom on a kitchen towel to absorb any moisture. Gently stir with a rubber spatula until smooth, returning to the heat briefly if lumps still remain.

Melted chocolate should look smooth and glossy and the temperature should never go above 115°F. Keep an eye on the sides of the bowl for telltale signs of scorching. As chocolate gets too hot, it will start darkening and losing its sheen around the edges. If the temperature goes above 120°F, the chocolate will separate and burn. If you suspect your chocolate may be burnt, the only thing to do is taste. Unfortunately, all you can do is toss out burnt chocolate, since there is no bringing it back.

combining melted chocolate

Butter, eggs, and other ingredients being added to melted chocolate should be at room temperature, since extreme heat or cold can shock the chocolate. Heat causes the cocoa butter and solids to separate; cold causes chocolate to harden into lumps.

{what to serve with chocolate desserts}

Once you have moved beyond ice-cold milk, the perfect beverage to complement a fine chocolate dessert is strong, dark coffee, preferably espresso. In my experience, teas are not an easy match for chocolate. A clean, dry, effervescent Champagne, though, can be perfect. Small sips of liqueurs can also be delightful with a rich chocolate dessert, but avoid going too sweet in your selection. I like a good tawny Port, brandy, or Cognac, Muscat, or a Banyuls. Taste and experiment to discover what works for you.

Chopping chocolate

chopping chocolate

To chop chocolate, the best tool is a long serrated knife. Starting on a corner of a block or square, shave ¼-inch-thick slices along the diagonal. The chocolate will naturally break into shards as you cut. Keep turning the square to work evenly off all the corners.

Pistoles are small disks of chocolate. Until recently, they have been primarily available to pastry chefs and chocolatiers, but these wafers of pure chocolate are now becoming easier to find. Their small, uniform size eliminates the need for chopping.

how to store chocolate

Chocolate should be kept in its wrapper and/or box and stored in a cool, dry, dark place. If storing an opened bar, wrap in its paper and then in a sealed plastic bag. The best storage temperature is 62 to 70°F. I do not recommend refrigeration because the condensation that occurs can result in sugar bloom (or grains on the surface). If you live in a hot place without air conditioning, however, there may be no option. Chocolate melts in the low nineties—a pleasure when it's in your mouth and a potential disaster in a very hot kitchen.

The whitish color that can rise to the top on chocolate is called fat bloom. It means the cocoa butter has separated and risen to the top due to heat. As unappealing as it looks, the final taste is not affected, because when the chocolate is melted, the cocoa butter will be redistributed throughout the chocolate.

how to make chocolate curls

To make large chocolate curls for decorating the tops of cakes, you need a large block of chocolate and a chef's knife. The chocolate should be at room temperature. Position it at

Large chocolate curls   *Small chocolate curls*

the edge of a work counter so the length is perpendicular to the table's edge. Standing over the chocolate, you want to be able to stabilize it with your body.

Holding the top of the blade with one hand at either end, not on the handle, position the sharp edge at between a 90 and 45 degree angle, slanting toward you. Firmly push down, dragging the blade forward to shave thin curls. Pick up the curls with a pastry scraper, since they easily melt, and transfer to the cake or reserve on a sheet of parchment.

For smaller curls use a small block of chocolate and a paring knife or a sharp vegetable peeler, holding the bar upright and scraping down. Or you can use a thin teaspoon. With the chocolate bar on a counter, holding the spoon horizontally, with the edge of the teaspoon bowl in one hand and the handle in the other, position the spoon at no more than a 45-degree angle slanting toward you. Firmly push down, pulling the spoon forward, to shave small, thin curls. This spoon technique is easiest with white chocolate.

how to grate chocolate

I like to use a handheld microplaner for grating chocolate for decorating. The fine side of a box grater is also good. It's best to grate chocolate just before using, as the fine pieces can easily lose their shape.

chocolate kitchen clean-up

At times the fun of working in the chocolate kitchen can be diminished by the sheer messiness of it all. With all that pouring, glazing, and finger dipping you're bound to start noticing that chocolate leaves big brown stains. My solution at home is to stock the kitchen with dark brown or black kitchen towels and black aprons, much better than white for hiding the brown. To remove chocolate stains, try soaking with liquid dishwasher detergent before tossing in the washing machine.

time, temperature, and movement explored

When time, temperature, and movement are perfectly orchestrated, the resulting chocolate desserts should have the power to bring even the most hardened adult to his or her knees. Why else would a grown woman spend so much time in the kitchen? A few secrets revealed:

time: One of the qualities I look for in aspiring chocolatiers is patience. Chocolate does not like to be rushed, so when we talk about time it's all about melting chocolate slowly, stirring slowly and gently, and the ability to wait hours, or even a day, for flavors to mellow and textures to change.

temperature: At the risk of scaring off newcomers I can't emphasize enough the importance of temperature to coaxing the very best out of chocolate. The general laws of chemistry dictate that heat will always turn chocolate into liquid and cold will turn it solid. Where important, the exact temperatures appear in the recipes, but here is a chart of the most important temperatures:

Chocolate storage	62 to 70°F
Melting dark chocolate	108 to 115°F
Tempering dark chocolate	88 to 90°F
Pouring chocolate butter glaze	80 to 85°F
Pouring ganache glaze	80 to 85°F

movement: Movement around melted chocolate should always be slow and gentle, stirring with a rubber spatula. Movement is what cools melted chocolate and thickens it while evenly distributing those all-important cocoa crystals for utter smoothness. A chocolate and cream ganache that is left untouched for many hours, like the truffle centers, will eventually thicken, developing a very deep, rich chocolate flavor. With a ganache for glazing, there is no need to wait so long. Thirty minutes, with a stir here and there, will bring the chocolate to perfect consistency. Each recipe contains the specifics.

OTHER INGREDIENTS

It takes only a few ingredients to achieve perfect chocolate desserts. Most of these recipes are a variation on the theme of butter, cream, sugar, eggs, and chocolate, with maybe a pinch of vanilla or nuts.

butter

All of the recipes in the book were developed with fresh unsalted butter. A premium-quality supermarket brand is fine. I do enjoy fine, imported high-butterfat brands for table butter, but have found some to be too strong and overpowering for my chocolates and chocolate desserts.

❧ hosting a chocolate tasting ❧

Since preferences are very personal, taking the time to discern the subtle differences among chocolates is a prerequisite for the serious aficionado. Each manufacturer has a unique style that can best be understood by tasting samples back to back. It's great fun to invite over a group of friends who are as dedicated to the pursuit of pure chocolate knowledge as you are. Then you can share your thoughts and impressions. And no one can accuse you of hoarding your chocolates.

Have on hand a selection of plain, thin bars meant for eating. They could range in cacao content from about 40 percent for a premium milk chocolate to about 70 percent or a bit higher for a fine bittersweet.

Set up a table with sheets of parchment paper and arrange the unwrapped bars according to cacao percentages, ranging from the most bitter to the least. Unlike wine tasting, where you move from light to dark (or white to red), with chocolate you begin with the darkest, most bitter chocolates and work your way down the scale. Pitchers of room-temperature water are best for palate cleansing between tastes. Strong flavors like coffee would cloud your ability to truly taste. The mood will be elevated enough from the chocolate.

As the host, it is your duty to demonstrate proper technique. Break off a small piece of chocolate. Listen for a clean, sharp snap and observe the surface sheen before bringing that piece up to your nose, warming it between your fingers, and inhaling. The initial aroma should be of chocolate, pleasant and mild, followed by secondary aromas of flowers, fruit, and spice. Now the moment of truth! Pop the piece into your mouth and let it melt on your tongue.

As the chocolate melts and coats your mouth, think about the flavor and textures you're experiencing that are truly much more than sweetness. You might want to keep a notebook of your impressions of aroma, texture, "mouth-feel," chocolate flavor, and aftertaste. Most important, stock up on a few of your new favorite bars for your private nibbling stash.

The key to baking with butter is to follow the directions about temperature carefully. If the butter is described as "room temperature," it should be very soft and warm, ideally about 70°F. At home, I like to take butter out of the refrigerator the night before to soften, or leave it out on a counter for about six hours. In a rush, cold butter can be softened by breaking into pieces and beating with the paddle on the mixer for about 8 minutes before starting the recipe.

sugars

granulated: If the list calls for sugar, use granulated white cane sugar. I prefer cane sugar because it dissolves quickly and caramelizes best. Look for the words "pure cane sugar" on the label. The C&H brand is widely available.

confectioners' or powdered: Fine confectioners' or powdered sugar is granulated sugar that has been ground to a fine white powder. A small amount of cornstarch has been added to prevent lumps from forming.

brown sugar: Brown sugar, or sugar to which molasses has been added, is available at the market in light and dark varieties. All of the recipes were developed using light-brown sugar, but feel free to experiment with other types—just avoid crystallized brown sugars like turbinado because they won't dissolve in the same way. Store in an airtight container in the pantry.

crystal sugar: Decorative or crystal sugars that do not dissolve in baking are used to add a finishing touch or crunch to a cookie or pastry. King Arthur's catalog and specialty grocers stock a wide variety.

heavy cream

Purchase heavy whipping cream for the best whipped cream. The recipes were tested with 40 percent butterfat, for the best mounding.

eggs

The recipes are made with "large" size eggs from the supermarket.

flour

All of the recipes calling for flour were developed with unbleached all-purpose flour, unless noted.

cake flour

Cake flour is lower in protein and gluten and produces a soft, tender crumb. I call for it in many of the cakes and tortes and also prefer it for tart crusts. It is available in a box in the baking section of the supermarket. Do not substitute whole-wheat pastry flour.

nuts

Always buy the best, freshest nuts available. As a general rule I find that whole nuts or halves are of better quality than smaller pieces. Store nuts in airtight ziplock bags in the freezer and warm the nuts through before baking by placing on a tray in a 300°F oven for about 10 minutes. Toast just until their fragrance is released, except for macadamias.

To toast unsalted macadamias, bake in a 300°F oven 10 to 12 minutes, until light blond in color. Search through the cooled nuts and pull out and discard any that are dark brown. Their taste will be off.

almond flour

Almond flour, called for in many of the tortes, is a meal made of blanched ground almonds. It's easy to make at home and extra can always be stored in the freezer for future recipes. You may also find it in bulk at specialty grocers.

To make almond flour, purchase slivered or whole blanched almonds. Working in small batches, with the food processor never more than half full, start by pulsing until large chunks are formed. Then process 15 to 20 seconds, until a fine meal is formed, being careful not to overprocess. As with all nuts, overprocessing will turn almonds into an oily paste or "butter." As a general rule, the following equivalents apply:

4 ounces almonds = 1 cup almond flour

1 ounce almonds = ¼ cup almond flour

1.3 ounces almonds = ⅓ cup almond flour

hazelnut paste

Similar to peanut butter, hazelnut paste is made of pure roasted hazelnuts. It is available in natural-food markets in the nut-butter section.

almond paste

Almond paste, not the same thing as marzipan, is a paste of ground almonds and sugar. Look for one with less than 25 percent sugar for a good almond flavor. It can be found in tubes and cans in the baking section of the supermarket. Once opened, wrap the remaining portion well in foil and store in the refrigerator for as long as two months.

salt

I recommend kosher salt for baking.

gianduja

Gianduja, beloved in Italy and Switzerland, is chocolate blended with finely ground hazelnuts. The variety that I use throughout the book is dark milk chocolate blended with hazelnuts. It can be found in specialty food stores or grocers. Each recipe supplies a formula for substituting milk chocolate and hazelnut paste if gianduja is not available.

dried fruits

I recommend visiting the bulk bins of your local grocer or natural food store for the best selection of plump, dried fruits. I'm a big fan of all the new fruits being dried: sour cherries, raspberries, mango, etc.

key lime juice

If you can't find fresh key limes, substitute an unsweetened brand found in the fruit juice section of your market. I prefer key limes to ordinary limes for their fuller, rounder flavor.

instant coffee

Most of the coffee-infused recipes in the book call for either brewed espresso (instant espresso powder may be used) or freeze-dried instant coffee. Always let the brewed espresso cool to room temperature before combining with other ingredients.

After experimenting with several brands of instant, I discovered that organic freeze-dried offers the best flavor. When instant espresso powder is called for, I use the Medaglia D'Oro brand.

EQUIPMENT

I'm a firm believer in the low-tech kitchen; still it does take a few good tools to make a great chocolate dessert.

heavy-duty mixer

A heavy-duty tabletop mixer with two mixing bowls will vastly improve your baking life. The second bowl is a great convenience when you have batter in one bowl and the egg whites still need to be whipped. All of these recipes were tested at home with a KitchenAid model K5A that I've had for years. If you use a similar model, the suggested times for beating and whipping offer accurate guidelines.

The recipes can also be made by hand or with a hand-held mixer, though it does take a bit of elbow grease and more time. As a general rule, increase the guidelines for time and use your senses to judge readiness—cream until perfectly smooth, whip until soft peaks form, etc.

kitchen scales

You'll need a scale for weighing the chocolate. I am partial to the digital kind, though any accurate scale will do.

thermometers

I know the thought of running around the kitchen with a thermometer may seem less than romantic, but for the very best results when working with chocolate I do recommend you have one available. If you first learn how to make a ganache or glaze using a thermometer as your guide, you stand a much better chance of knowing what to look for when you are ready to rely on your senses.

A good Insta-Read thermometer by Taylor costs about ten dollars in the supermarket or hardware store. Since they are delicate, you want to check accuracy every so often. Just plunge in boiling water to calibrate to a reading of 212°F. The little screw on top can be turned to adjust. See page 16 for the key temperatures for melting and handling chocolate.

rubber spatulas

I have a collection of rubber spatulas for my home baking—all different sizes. They really are the best for folding batters without beating in air, scraping down the sides of mixing bowls, and stirring chocolate. The new heat-resistant rubber spatulas are great. They're perfect for melting chocolate and making caramel, since they don't burn or melt over high heat. All of the kitchenware shops sell them.

metal spatulas

You'll need at least one long, thin metal spatula, about 8 inches long by 1 inch wide, for cake making. In the pastry kitchen these are used for spreading glazes and frosting, smoothing tops, and lifting a finished cake. I like to have a few different sizes—small for bite-size cookies, candies, and petit fours; and larger ones for handling and moving substantial cakes.

Offset spatulas, with their blades a step down from their handles, are especially handy for leveling the batter in a sheet pan. Just rest the blade along the edges and skim the blade across. I look for thin flexible blades when purchasing spatulas and suggest that you purchase two, one offset and one straight, when you are getting started.

to transfer a cake using a long spatula: Slide the blade a few inches in between the cake board (see page 26) and rack. Using the spatula to lift the cake slightly, slide your other hand, palm up, under the cake to lift and support. Holding the cake up in the air, you can scrape any excess glaze off the bottom edge with the spatula. Lower the cake by lowering your hand over the serving platter. When the cake is an inch or two over the plate, slide the spatula back underneath and remove your hand. Slowly lower the cake into position and slide out the spatula.

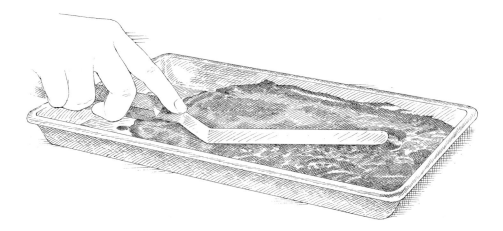

Offset spatula used for leveling batter in a sheet pan

silpat

These miraculous silicone-treated rubber mats, made to fit standard baking sheets, are totally nonstick and amazingly durable. They replace parchment paper or the need to coat cookie sheets, and they are excellent for pouring hot caramel for decorating. I paid fifteen dollars for the one I have at home and it has lasted forever. Just handwash with soapy water between jobs.

baking pans and sheets

All of the recipes in the book can be made with a small collection of pans available at most cookware shops.

9-inch round fluted tart pan with removable bottom: Available at cookware shops; the bottoms may be used as cake boards.

9-by-13-inch sheet pans, also called quarter sheets or jelly-roll pans: Sheet pans look like cookie sheets with 1-inch-deep sides all around. They are perfect for the brownie, rolled cake, and sheet cake recipes and also may be used as cookie sheets or for toasting nuts. Look for them at any cookware store or online at Williams-Sonoma and Sur La Table, where they are often sold in sets of two.

9-inch fluted tart pan

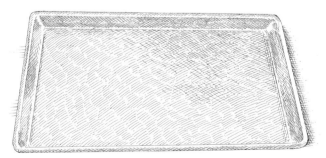

Quarter-sheet pan

9-inch round cake pans: These round pans with 2-inch-deep sides are available at cookware shops. Any of the batters for one 9-inch round cake can be divided in half to make two 6-inch round cakes.

9-inch round French flare–sided cake pans: For many of the dense European-style tortes in the book I recommend flare-sided cake pans, available at cake supply shops and Sur La Table. The slightly graduated thin sides help naturally leavened batters attain better height and, when inverted, the edges are easier to glaze because the glaze slides down a slight slope, not a straight side. By all means, do not deny yourself a luscious-sounding cake because you don't have a flared pan. The difference between a cake baked in a pan with straight rather than flared sides is minimal. No one will be the wiser. On the other hand, as you strive for perfection, you may want to purchase one to see what all the fuss is about.

OPTIONAL:

9-inch round springform pan: These traditional round pans have removable sides. Often used for cheesecakes, they are good for making some of the chilled, molded desserts. Available at cookware shops.

cookie sheet: Real cookie sheets are perfectly flat, without a raised edge to obstruct cookie viewing and lifting. I prefer to use the heavy half-sheet pans.

half-sheet pan: Twice the size of a quarter sheet, these 18-by-13-inch sheet pans with 1-inch-deep sides are good for baking larger sheet cakes. Sold at most cookware shops.

parchment paper

Parchment paper, or paper treated with a silicone coating, should be a staple in your kitchen if you do much baking. Professionals use it for lining cake pans and cookie sheets. It can also be used as a flexible surface for spreading tempered chocolate or making decorations and for improvising a pastry cone for piping. It is sold in rolls at the supermarket and in specialty shops. Precut parchment circles that fit standard-size cake pans are available at specialty shops and by mail order.

to make a parchment pastry cone: Cut out of parchment paper a triangle with a 17-inch-long base and 12-inch sides. Holding the center pointing up in your left hand, take the right corner in your right hand and turn it clockwise, bringing the point up to meet the center point at a 45-degree angle. Tuck it in your left hand.

Then take the left corner in your right hand and turn it counterclockwise until the point meets the other side, making a 90-degree angle at the center. The two points should line up in the center with no more than a pinpoint of light showing in the tip of the cone. Pull both ends up slightly to tighten the hole.

To secure, overlap the ends slightly to make a strong seam and make several narrow folds at the top, pressing with your fingers so the creases will hold. Each cone holds about 3 tablespoons of filling. Since paper cones are delicate, I recommend having a few ready when you begin decorating. Precut paper triangles and cones may be available at well-stocked cake supply stores.

Forming a parchment paper cone

pastry bags

Pastry bags and tips can be intimidating for the new baker, though, once again, all it takes is practice and patience. Old-fashioned plastic-coated fabric can be easily washed and used again. I recommend starting with three tips: one star and two rounds (¼-inch and ½-inch). Because they are more durable, pastry bags are preferable to parchment cones for heavier fillings or larger quantities.

to fill a pastry bag: Place your selected tip in the small opening at the narrow end of the bag. Twist the fabric above the tip to temporarily plug the hole while you fill the bag. Fold the top of the bag over and spoon in the filling so the bag is no more than two-thirds full. Fold up and twist to close the top of the bag. You are ready to pipe. Support the bag with two hands: The bottom guides the tip, while the top presses and releases the filling.

cake boards

Once you discover these precut corrugated cardboard circles, you'll wonder how you lived without them. Cut to fit the standard-size cake pans (8-, 9-, and 10-inch circles) these sturdy sheets support your cake's bottom as it takes on its fillings and glazes. We use a single-edged razor blade or serrated knife blade to trim down sheets to fit special logs and squares.

mixing bowls

A graduated set of stainless-steel mixing bowls is a good investment for all of your cooking. For baking and melting chocolate, they are the best. Lightweight stainless steel adjusts quickly to heat and cold and is easier to handle than heavy pottery.

cooling and pouring racks

Many of the recipes call for a cooling or pouring rack that fits inside a 9-by-13-inch pan for catching drippy glazes. Any footed rack that allows air to circulate below is fine.

whisks

There is no one best size for a whisk. Just look for a flexible whisk with many spokes that feels comfortable in your hand. Smaller hands call for smaller whisks.

knives

The one knife that I could not live without in the pastry kitchen is one with a long serrated blade. I use it for slicing and trimming cake layers, chopping chocolate, and, in a pinch, the teeth can be used to comb a pattern in a glaze. A thin bladed paring knife is also indispensable. It is called for throughout the book to remove cakes from their pans. I also use an 8" chef's knife to chop and slice most anything, and if your blade has a bit of a flex, it is the perfect knife for making chocolate curls.

cake tester

You can choose a metal cake tester purchased at a kitchen supply shop or a clean dry toothpick; either will suffice.

amazing cookies and brownies

⋅{ truffle brownies }⋅

If you agree with most children that nuts just get in the way of a good brownie, these moist, dense chocolate cakes are for you. At the store, we wrap each individually and stack on the counter for those who need a quick treat to eat in the car or to tuck into a special lunchbox. The idea of combining two types of chocolate for a deeper, more complex flavor came from my son, Dylan, a chocolate purist of the first order. This really is a cross between a brownie and a truffle—it is so, so rich!

makes 24 large brownies or 48 miniatures

8 ounces bittersweet chocolate, finely chopped

2 ounces unsweetened chocolate, finely chopped

½ pound (2 sticks) unsalted butter, room temperature

1 cup packed brown sugar

½ cup sugar

6 large eggs, room temperature

2 teaspoons pure vanilla extract

1 cup flour

Position a rack in the middle of the oven and preheat the oven to 325°F. Lightly butter a 9-by-13-inch sheet pan, or quarter-sheet pan.

In a double boiler over simmering water combine the chocolates. Remove when nearly melted and continue stirring until smooth. Set aside to cool.

In a mixer with a paddle attachment, beat the butter and both sugars at medium speed until light, 5 to 6 minutes.

Add the eggs, one at a time, beating well after each addition and scraping down the sides of the bowl. Add the vanilla and continue beating until the mixture is smooth and light, 2 to 3 minutes. Pour in the cooled chocolate and mix well. If the butter begins to melt when the chocolate is added, stop pouring and let the chocolate cool further. The finished mixture should be glossy and smooth.

With a rubber spatula, gently fold in the flour until all traces of white have disappeared. Be careful not to overmix.

Pour the batter into the prepared pan and bake 30 minutes, or until the crust is dull on top and a cake tester inserted in the center comes out with dark, wet crumbs on it.

Let cool in the pan about 1 hour. Cut into squares and remove with a spatula. Store brownies in sealed plastic containers for as long as a week, or freeze.

Serving Suggestions: Brownies are delicious topped with a scoop of ice cream or any of the sauces in the Silken Dessert Sauces chapter.

white-chocolate chunk brownies

These buttery yellow bars packed with white-chocolate chunks and toasted pecans taste like a rich, chewy cookie in a pan—a sure trip to heaven for the white-chocolate lover. Use a high-quality white chocolate and you won't be disappointed!

makes 24 brownies or 48 miniatures

1½ cups pecan halves

1 pound white chocolate

½ pound (2 sticks) unsalted butter, room temperature, cut in tablespoon-size pieces

3 large eggs

¾ cup sugar

1 teaspoon pure vanilla extract

1½ cups cake flour, sifted then measured

Position a rack in the middle of the oven and preheat the oven to 325°F.

Lightly butter a 9-by-13-inch sheet pan, or quarter-sheet pan.

Place the pecans on an uncoated baking sheet and toast in the oven for 10 minutes, or until their fragrance is released. Let cool, then roughly chop into pieces no larger than ½ inch. Set aside.

Divide the white chocolate in half. Finely chop one half for melting, and roughly chop the other portion into ¼-inch chunks. Set aside for chips.

Melt the finely chopped white chocolate in a double boiler over low heat. Remove when nearly melted and continue stirring until smooth, about 100°F. Add the softened butter. Set aside, without stirring.

In a mixer fitted with a whisk attachment, whip together the eggs, sugar, and vanilla until light and very fluffy, 3 to 5 minutes. Add the chocolate and butter mixture and whisk on low speed until combined, stopping to scrape the bowl several times.

Remove the bowl from the mixer and fold in the flour until no traces remain. Fold in the white chocolate chunks and toasted pecans. The batter will be quite thick. Evenly spread into the prepared pan. Bake for 35 to 40 minutes, until the top is completely golden brown.

Let cool in the pan about 1 hour. Cut into squares and remove with a spatula. Store brownies in sealed plastic containers, or freeze.

❧ gold bar brownies ❧

As demand started to increase for our first adult candy bar, the Gold Bar, we were faced with the pleasant problem of what to do with the odds and ends left on the trays after the bars were cut. I know it's hard to imagine, but even chocolate professionals have to stop eating chocolate eventually. When the volume got too great to distribute as samples, we tried selling bags of remnants for nibbling—and then lightning struck! Someone came up with the idea of folding the pieces into a brownie, creating the sensational Gold Bar Brownie—an over-the-top chocolate brownie shot through with gooey caramel and almonds.

This version, developed for the home baker without an endless supply of broken Gold Bars, is the next evolution of that toothsome concept. You can make the caramel sauce several weeks in advance, or purchase a good prepared sauce. The results are always awe inspiring.

makes 24 brownies or 48 miniatures

1 cup Caramel Sauce (page 177) or storebought

8 ounces (1⅔ cups) whole almonds

1 pound (16 ounces) semisweet chocolate

1½ ounces unsweetened chocolate, finely chopped

1 stick plus 2 tablespoons unsalted butter, room temperature

¾ cup plus 2 tablespoons packed brown sugar

⅔ cup sugar

1½ teaspoons pure vanilla extract

¾ teaspoon instant espresso powder

3 large eggs

1¾ cups cake flour, sifted then measured

Position a rack in the middle of the oven and preheat the oven to 325°F.

Lightly butter a 9-by-13-inch sheet pan, or quarter-sheet pan.

Have ready the Caramel Sauce. The sauce can be made as much as a month in advance. It can be used cold, directly from the refrigerator.

Place the almonds on another baking sheet and toast in the oven for 10 minutes,

(continued)

or until their fragrance is released. Let cool, then roughly chop into ¼-inch pieces. Set aside.

Finely chop 12 ounces of the semisweet chocolate for melting. Chop the remaining 4 ounces of semisweet into ¼-inch chunks for chips.

Melt the finely chopped semisweet and unsweetened chocolates in a double boiler over low heat. Remove when nearly melted and continue stirring until smooth, about 100°F.

In a mixer fitted with a paddle attachment, beat together the butter and two sugars until light and very fluffy, 3 to 5 minutes. In a small bowl, stir together the vanilla and the espresso powder.

Add to the butter mixture and beat to combine. Add the eggs, one at a time, beating well between additions and scraping the bowl several times. Pour in the melted chocolate and beat to combine.

Remove the bowl from the mixer and fold in the sifted flour by hand until no traces of white remain. Fold in the toasted almonds and the 4 ounces semisweet chocolate chunks. The batter will be quite thick. Evenly spread the batter in the prepared pan.

Spoon the cold Caramel Sauce in tablespoon-size dollops over the top. Using a table knife drawn through the batter, swirl the caramel into the batter to marbelize. Bake for 45 minutes. When tested with a toothpick in the brownie portion (not the caramel), it will have moist crumbs.

Let cool in the pan 1 hour. Cut into squares and remove with a spatula. Store brownies in sealed plastic containers as long as a week, or freeze.

❧ chocolate meringues ❧

Solid bits of bittersweet chocolate ratchet up the chocolate intensity of these crisp, light brown meringues. Light as clouds, meringues are always a good addition to a sweet tray to balance the richer items. Meringues can be dressed up by dipping in tempered chocolate (see page 190) or making little sandwiches filled with ganache. Plan ahead since they do need to dry in the oven. The best time for baking is after dinner when the day's cooking is done.

makes about 40 cookies

4 large egg whites (4 fluid ounces)

1 cup sugar

1 tablespoon plus 1½ teaspoons Dutch-processed cocoa powder

4 ounces bittersweet chocolate (preferably 70% cacao), very finely chopped (no pieces larger than ⅛ inch)

Position a rack in the middle of the oven and preheat the oven to 200°F. Have ready 2 parchment- or Silpat-lined cookie sheets and a large, pastry bag fitted with a large, ¾-inch star tip (Ateco #9848).

In a mixer fitted with a whisk attachment begin whipping the egg whites on medium-high speed, until foamy and white. Add half the sugar and continue whipping at high speed until stiff peaks are formed.

Sift together the remaining (½ cup) sugar and cocoa powder. Fold into the whipped whites using a rubber spatula. Then fold in the finely chopped chocolate.

Transfer the mixture to the pastry bag. Pipe into meringue peaks about 1½ inches at the base. Meringues can be positioned fairly close together since they will not spread.

Bake for 1 hour. Then turn the oven off, leaving cookies in the oven overnight or until crisp, about 6 hours. Store in a dry, airtight container up to about a week.

❧{ chocolate wafers }❧

This versatile cookie dough makes an exceptionally crisp cookie and a tart shell (page 222) with unmistakable deep dark chocolate flavor. A little tip for keeping the dough nice and dark is to dust the rolling surface and pin with a mixture of half cocoa, half flour. Bake up batches and use chocolate wafers to make the Ultimate Ice-Cream Sandwiches on page 150 or our version of the classic Ice-Box Cake (page 154) from the fifties. makes 24 cookies

1½ sticks (12 tablespoons) unsalted butter, room temperature

1 cup sugar

⅔ cup dark Dutch-processed cocoa powder, sifted

1 large egg

1½ teaspoons pure vanilla extract

1¼ cups flour

In a mixer with a paddle attachment, cream the butter and sugar on medium-high speed until fluffy, about 4 minutes.

Add the cocoa powder and mix on low speed until well combined. Scrape down the sides of the mixing bowl.

Add the egg and vanilla and blend thoroughly, scraping down the sides of the mixing bowl. Add the flour. Mix on low speed until the dough begins to hold together. Wrap the dough in plastic wrap and chill until firm, about 4 hours or overnight.

To bake, position an oven rack in the middle of the oven and preheat the oven to 325°F. Line a cookie sheet or two with parchment paper or Silpats.

Working quickly, on a lightly floured surface roll half the dough into a 12-by-12-inch square, about ⅛ inch thick. Using a 3¼-inch round cookie cutter, cut out about 12 cookies. With a metal spatula, transfer to a lined cookie sheet. Pierce each cookie with the tines of a fork several times. Bake for 8 to 10 minutes, until slightly dull on top. Transfer to racks to cool. They will crisp as they cool.

Repeat with the remaining dough, gathering the scraps together and gently kneading into a second batch. Store in an airtight container as long as 1 week.

❈{ chocolate sablés }❈

These classic refrigerator butter cookies bake up slightly crisp with a soft interior. They have a delightful crumble, enhanced by the potato starch, and as you might expect, they have that extra chocolate flavor that I can't do without. Stock your freezer with a roll for chocolate emergencies.

makes 60 to 75 cookies

8 ounces semisweet chocolate, finely chopped

½ pound (2 sticks) unsalted butter, room temperature

1 cup sugar

1 large egg

1 teaspoon pure vanilla extract

1 cup cake flour, sifted then measured

1 cup potato starch flour

½ cup Dutch-processed cocoa powder

pinch of salt

½ cup crystal sugar for decorating

In the top of a double boiler or in a bowl over simmering water, melt the chocolate. Remove from the heat when the chocolate is nearly melted and stir until smooth. Set aside to cool, returning to the double boiler only briefly if the chocolate begins to set up.

In a mixer fitted with the paddle attachment, beat the butter at medium speed until smooth and pale. Add the sugar and continue beating, scraping down the sides of the bowl often, until the mixture is completely smooth, 3 to 5 minutes total. Beat in the egg and vanilla until blended.

Pour in the melted chocolate and mix at medium-low speed just until blended, scraping down the sides of the bowl several times.

In another bowl, with a fork mix together the cake flour, potato flour, cocoa powder, and salt. Add to the chocolate mixture and mix at low speed just until blended, trying not to overmix.

Put the bowl of dough in the refrigerator and chill for 10 to 20 minutes, until firm enough to handle but not too stiff.

Transfer the dough to a lightly floured surface. By hand, press the dough into a log about 15 inches long and 2½ inches in diameter. (If the dough is too tacky, loosely wrap in a sheet of plastic wrap to form the roll.)

Spread the crystal sugar on a baking tray. Place the log (with plastic wrap removed) in the sugar and roll to evenly coat all surfaces except the ends. Wrap well in plastic wrap and chill until firm, at least 4 hours or up to 3 days. The log can also be frozen.

to bake the cookies

Position 2 racks in the middle of the oven and preheat the oven to 350°F. Have ready 2 cookie sheets lined with parchment paper or Silpats.

Remove the dough from the refrigerator and let sit on the counter for about 10 minutes, until warm enough to slice evenly. Using a thin-bladed chef's knife, cut the log into ¼-inch slices. Transfer the slices to the cookie sheets, leaving a 1-inch space between each.

Bake for 10 to 12 minutes, until the tops are dull. Transfer to racks to cool. Store in an airtight container as long as a week.

{ cookie pointers }

Cookies are a great place to begin your baking career. The best advice I can give you is to beat the butter and sugar longer than you think necessary, until there is absolutely not a grain of sugar to be seen or felt.

To improve even the simplest chocolate-chip cookie recipe, substitute hand-chopped chunks of a fine semi-sweet or bittersweet chocolate for the mass-produced morsels.

❧ pure chocolate-chunk cookies ❧

If traditional chocolate-chip cookies just don't do it for you these days, these dark-chocolate cookies may be just what you're looking for. They're soft, chewy, and chocolate through and through, without a nut in sight to sully their sheer chocolatey-ness. For a complete chocolate meltdown moment, you owe it to yourself (and anyone else in the house) to taste one straight from the oven, while the bittersweet chunks are still warm and oozing.

makes 3 dozen big cookies

12 ounces semisweet chocolate, finely chopped

1½ ounces unsweetened chocolate, finely chopped

1 stick plus 2 tablespoons unsalted butter, room temperature

¾ cup plus 2 tablespoons brown sugar

⅔ cup sugar

1½ teaspoons pure vanilla extract

3 large eggs

1¾ cups cake flour, sifted then measured

8 ounces bittersweet chocolate, cut in ¼-inch chunks

Position a rack in the middle of the oven and preheat the oven to 325°F. Line 2 cookie sheets with parchment paper or Silpats.

In a double boiler melt the semisweet and unsweetened chocolates over low heat. Remove the top part of the boiler when the chocolate is nearly melted and stir until smooth, about 100°F. Set aside.

In a mixer fitted with a paddle attachment, beat together the butter, two sugars, and vanilla until light and very fluffy, 3 to 5 minutes. Beat in the eggs, one at a time, stopping several times to scrape the bowl. Pour in the melted chocolate and mix to combine.

Fold in the sifted flour by hand until no traces of white remain. Fold in the bittersweet chocolate chunks. The batter will be quite thick. Chill for 1 hour.

Using a scoop or large spoon, scoop 2 tablespoons of dough for each cookie and drop onto the lined cookie sheets, leaving about 2 inches of space between the cookies. (The cookies will spread to about 3 inches in diameter.) Slightly flatten with your fingers and immediately place in the oven. The cookie dough should still be cold when baked.

Bake for 12 to 14 minutes, or until cracked and puffed on top. The insides should remain moist. Let cool on sheets about 10 minutes. Transfer to racks to completely cool. Store in an airtight container as long as 1 week.

VARIATION

For 6 dozen smaller cookies, use 1 tablespoon of dough per cookie and bake 8 to 10 minutes.

chocolate almond macaroons

Traditional French macaroons are crisp on the outside, moist and chewy on the inside, and fragrant with almonds. Unlike their coconut haystack cousins, these sophisticates bake up flat, like chubby chocolate wafers. They are delightful eaten plain. Sandwiched with a rich chocolate ganache, however, they reach for greatness.   makes about 18 sandwich cookies or 36 singles

½ recipe Dark Chocolate Truffle Filling (page 216)

10 ounces almond paste, room temperature, cut in small pieces

¾ cup plus 2 tablespoons sugar

3 tablespoons Dutch-processed cocoa powder

¼ cup plus 2 tablespoons almond flour (1⅓ ounces slivered blanched almonds, finely ground)

3 large egg whites (3 fluid ounces)

The day before baking the cookies, prepare the Dark Chocolate Truffle Filling.

Position 2 racks in the middle of the oven and preheat the oven to 325°F. Line 2 cookie sheets with parchment paper or Silpats.

In a mixer fitted with the paddle attachment, cream together the almond paste, sugar, cocoa powder, and almond flour until smooth.

Add the egg whites, one at a time, beating well and scraping down the bowl between additions. Mix until smooth and uniform.

Transfer the mixture to a pastry bag fitted with a large (½-inch) round tip (#808). Holding the pastry bag vertical to the prepared cookie sheet, pipe about 36 disks, 1¾ inches round and ⅓ inch high.

For a smoother finish, dampen a smooth cotton tea towel or napkin. Lightly pat the top of each macaroon to moisten.

Bake for 12 to 15 minutes, until puffed. Let cool on trays 10 minutes. Then transfer to racks to cool completely.

To form sandwiches, spread the bottoms of half the cooled cookies with about ½ teaspoon of ganache. Top with the bottom of a second macaroon to make a sandwich. Store in airtight containers as long as a week if totally dry.

white-chocolate coconut cream bars

I am so fond of traditional layered cookies like lemon bars or cheesecake squares that I thought long and hard about how best to showcase my favorite ingredient in a bar before taking the plunge. I think you'll approve of the spectacular results of months of research, not to mention cookie tasting. The bottom layer is a pressed crust of crumbly shortbread made with two kinds of chocolate, the middle layer is like a smooth, dense white-chocolate pudding laced with shredded coconut, and the top layer caps it all off with a roof of ultra-suave bittersweet ganache. Life—or at least a bar cookie—doesn't get much better than this. Plan on savoring such a rich cookie on its own, like a bar of candy. Any ice cream or sauce would be superfluous.

makes 24 bars

coconut cream filling

½ cup heavy cream

8 ounces white chocolate, finely chopped

1¼ ounces unsweetened finely shredded dried coconut

white-chocolate shortbread layer

4 ounces semisweet chocolate, finely chopped

6 ounces white chocolate, finely chopped

⅓ cup sugar

1 stick (8 tablespoons) unsalted butter, room temperature

2 cups cake flour, sifted then measured

dark ganache topping

½ cup heavy cream

3½ ounces semisweet chocolate, finely chopped

to make the filling

In a saucepan heat cream over medium-high heat just until it begins to simmer. Remove from the heat, add the white chocolate, and stir until smooth and melted. Stir in the coconut. Pour into a small bowl and cover with plastic wrap touching the top. Let sit at room temperature at least 3 but no longer than 24 hours.

to make the shortbread layer

Lightly butter a 9-by-13-inch sheet pan, or quarter-sheet pan.

(continued)

In a food processor fitted with a metal blade, pulse the semisweet chocolate for 1 minute. Place in a small bowl, removing any larger pieces, and reprocess briefly. (Be careful not to overprocess.) The finished chocolate should be ground to pieces about $\frac{1}{16}$ to $\frac{1}{8}$ inch. Set aside.

In a double boiler melt the white chocolate over low heat. Remove the top of the boiler when the chocolate is nearly melted and continue stirring until glossy and smooth. Set aside to cool slightly. Return to the double boiler only briefly if chocolate begins to set up.

In a mixer fitted with a paddle attachment, cream the sugar and butter on medium-high speed until light in color and fluffy, 3 to 5 minutes. Add the melted white chocolate and blend thoroughly on medium-high speed. Add the sifted cake flour and the processed dark chocolate. Mix on low speed until the dough begins to hold together. Remove from the mixing bowl and gently knead a few times to thoroughly mix.

Press the dough evenly into the bottom of the prepared pan. Refrigerate or freeze until firm.

to bake the bars

Position a rack in the middle of the oven and preheat the oven to 325°F.

Bake the chilled shortbread crust until lightly golden and slightly puffed, 25 minutes. Cool completely in the pan. If the base settles a bit in the center, do not worry. It will be perfect for holding the filling.

to assemble the bars

Place the coconut cream filling in the bowl of a heavy-duty mixer fitted with a paddle attachment, or use a hand mixer. Beat on medium speed, scraping the sides of the bowl several times, until the filling is lighter in both color and texture, less than 1 minute. Spread the filling evenly and smoothly over the baked cooled shortbread layer.

to make the ganache and finish the bars

In a pot heat the cream over medium-high heat until it begins to simmer. Remove from the heat and stir in the finely chopped chocolate until smooth. Let cool until about 80–85°F. Slowly pour over the coconut filling, spreading it evenly to the edges.

Let set at room temperature about 1 hour, or place in the refrigerator to cool quickly, about 20 minutes. To cut, score the filling with a sharp knife where you wish to cut. Then slice through the base with a long, sharp blade. Remove the bars with a spatula. Store in a sealed container in the refrigerator as long as a week.

chocolate tuile cups

Tuiles, the traditional French cookie cups for serving ice creams and mousses, are usually golden wafers. For the chocolate version, I added cocoa for a very thin, crisp, dark brown cookie with deep chocolate flavor—marvelous with all of the ice creams and sorbets starting on page 145. If you haven't already purchased a silicone baking sheet or Silpat, now may be the time. Thin tuiles will stick unmercifully to parchment paper, and if you bake directly on the baking sheet, be prepared to wash and dry between batches.

makes 24 to 32 cookies

1 cup plus 1 tablespoon sugar

¾ cup cake flour, sifted then measured

2 tablespoons Dutch-processed cocoa powder

3 egg whites (3 fluid ounces)

¾ stick (6 tablespoons) unsalted butter

Position a rack in the middle of the oven and preheat the oven to 350°F. Line a cookie sheet with a Silpat, or lightly coat with butter and dust with flour.

Sift together the sugar, cake flour, and cocoa into a mixing bowl. Stir in the egg whites with a wire whisk, not beating in air.

Melt the butter in a small saucepan over low heat. Add the hot butter to the bowl, whisking until smooth without beating in air. Cover and chill for 20 minutes.

Spoon rounded teaspoons of the cool batter onto the Silpat. Make each batch small,

about 3 cookies. Using the back of a tablespoon, spread the batter in a circular motion to form a thin 5-inch round circle.

Bake for 4 to 5 minutes. Tuiles should bubble slightly in baking and then fall flat on the cookie sheet when done. You may need to adjust the timing for these delicate cookies. If the first batch isn't crisp enough, bake a bit longer. Or if the cookies are too crisp to bend, reduce the time by a minute or 2. Meanwhile, arrange about 6 glasses with 2¼-inch round bases upside-down on a counter.

Working quickly, with a metal spatula lift each tuile from the pan and invert onto the bottom of a glass. Using a tea towel if necessary, gently press the warm tuile around the glass to form a cup. Let cool about a minute to crisp. Remove and store in an airtight container as long as a week.

chocolate madeleines

You're missing out on a truly great chocolate experience if you aren't baking these classic little French sponge cakes at home. But don't stay too close to the kitchen once they come out of the oven. Eaten while still warm, these soft, rich chocolate madeleines are addictive.

My daughter, Andrina, an MBA graduate and twenty-first-century noncook, tested this recipe to great acclaim—and her own amazement. Once she got past finding a pan, it was a breeze. She made some discoveries in the course of her recipe testing: The molds must be filled evenly so that all the little cookies are ready to come out of the oven at the exact same time; the pleasure of providing so much instant gratification is immeasurable; and her appetite for madeleines and cold milk runs deep. Just like her mother's.

makes 24 to 30 cookies

2 tablespoons room-temperature unsalted butter, for coating, plus 1½ sticks (12 tablespoons) unsalted butter

6 ounces semisweet chocolate, finely chopped

3 large eggs

½ cup plus 2 tablespoons sugar

1 teaspoon pure vanilla extract

1 cup cake flour, sifted then measured

½ teaspoon baking powder

¼ cup Dutch-processed cocoa powder

Generously rub the insides of 2 madeleine pans with the 2 tablespoons softened butter.

Melt the 1½ sticks of butter and set aside to cool partially.

In the top of a double boiler (or in a bowl over simmering water), melt the chocolate over low heat. Remove the top of the boiler when the chocolate is nearly melted and stir until smooth. Set aside to cool, returning to the double boiler only briefly if it begins to set up.

In a mixer fitted with the whisk attachment, whisk together the eggs and sugar on high speed until thick and pale yellow, 3 to 5 minutes. Whisk in the vanilla. Remove the bowl from the mixer and with a rubber spatula fold in the melted chocolate.

Sift together the cake flour, baking powder, and cocoa. Gently fold the dry ingredients into the chocolate mixture. Add the cooled melted butter. Fold until the batter is smooth and uniform. Cover and chill for 20 minutes.

To bake, position a rack in the middle of the oven and preheat the oven to 425°F.

Place the batter in a pastry bag fitted with a large (½-inch) round tip (#808). Holding the pastry bag vertical to the prepared pans, pipe into the molds until three-quarters full. The batter may also be spooned into the prepared pans, as evenly as possible for even baking.

Bake for 8 to 10 minutes, until cookies are peaked in the center and crisp on the outside. Immediately turn out onto a cooling rack. If you hesitate for more than a moment, the madeleines will stick to the pans like glue. Store madeleines (those that aren't immediately devoured) in an airtight container as long as 5 days.

{ tortes, with and without flour }

{ l'orange }

As soon as you cut a slice of L'Orange, the room fills with the most remarkable orange essence. This Viennese-style fruit-and-nut torte was always a popular choice at the shop, and it remains the most accessible of tortes. In fact, I like to recommend it to new bakers since there are no eggs to separate and very little that can go wrong. Unlike the other tortes with a perfectly smooth texture, L'Orange is pebbly with almonds. With its concentration of fruits and nuts it can stay moist on a counter for several days—though I doubt that it will last that long.

serves 12 to 16

6 ounces semisweet chocolate, finely chopped

2 oranges, preferably large navels with dark, rough-textured skin

1½ sticks (12 tablespoons) unsalted butter, room temperature

1 cup sugar

4 large eggs, room temperature

1⅔ cups (6⅔ ounces) almond flour (page 19)

1 recipe Chocolate Butter Glaze (page 214)

Position a rack in the middle of the oven and preheat the oven to 300°F.

Butter a 9-inch round cake pan (preferably flared) and line with a parchment circle.

In a double boiler melt the chocolate over low heat. Remove when nearly melted and continue stirring until smooth. Briefly return to the double boiler if it begins to thicken.

Wash the oranges. Using a fine grater or microplaner, finely grate the zest directly into the mixing bowl, so that all the fragrant orange oils are captured.

Add the butter and sugar to the orange zest in the bowl. Beat with the paddle attachment on medium-high speed until light in color, 3 to 5 minutes. Scrape down the sides of the bowl with a rubber spatula halfway through.

With the mixer on medium-high speed, begin adding the eggs slowly, one at a time. Continue beating until well mixed, about 3 minutes total. The beaten mixture will be lighter in color and will have increased in volume.

Remove the bowl from the mixer. Using a rubber spatula, fold in the almond flour. Then fold in the melted chocolate. Evenly spread the batter into the prepared pan.

Bake for 40 to 45 minutes, until puffed and domed in the center with a slight fracture 1 inch from the rim. The top will appear lighter in color. A cake tester inserted in the center will have a few moist crumbs. Allow cake to cool at room temperature in the pan for approximately 15 minutes.

To remove from pan, run a thin-bladed knife around the edges of the cake and invert onto a cardboard cake circle or metal tart-pan bottom. Chill completely. (The torte can be wrapped in plastic once cooled and placed in the freezer for up to a week prior to assembly.)

to finish the torte

Bring the torte to room temperature, unwrap it, and remove parchment paper. Trim uneven edges.

Have ready the Chocolate Butter Glaze.

Place the torte (on the cardboard cake circle or tart bottom) on a cooling rack positioned over a rimmed baking sheet. Beginning 1½ inches from the edge of the torte, slowly and evenly pour the glaze around the torte layer, making sure that the sides are sufficiently covered. Then pour the remaining glaze onto the center.

Working quickly, using a metal offset spatula, spread the glaze evenly over the top, letting the excess run down the sides.

Let set at room temperature until the glaze is slightly firm, about 5 minutes. Once set, slide an offset spatula under the cardboard circle, rotating the spatula to release any spots where the glaze has stuck to the rack. Carefully lift the torte and, supporting the cake's bottom with your free hand, slide it onto its serving plate. (See illustrations, next page.) Can be stored at room temperature up to 3 days, with cut edges protected.

creaming butter and sugar

The process of beating together butter and sugar is the key step to providing structure for uniform height and consistency. Take your time and do it right, and you will be rewarded with a beautiful cake every time. It's best to start with soft, pliable, room-temperature butter. In a heavy-duty mixer with a paddle attachment, beat the butter at medium speed until soft and fluffy. Reduce the speed to low, add the sugar, and keep beating until the sugar totally dissolves. You shouldn't see or feel any sugar granules when pinching a piece of batter between your fingers. It takes about 5 minutes to totally dissolve the sugar, but it is almost impossible to beat too long. (If you must start with cold butter, cut the stick into small pieces and beat to soften before adding the sugar.)

For some cakes or puddings, sugar and egg yolks, rather than butter, are beaten together. It's important to note that sugar and yolks left unmixed undergo a chemical reaction that "burns" the yolks, turning them hard and unmixable. You want to mix these two together as soon as they go in the bowl.

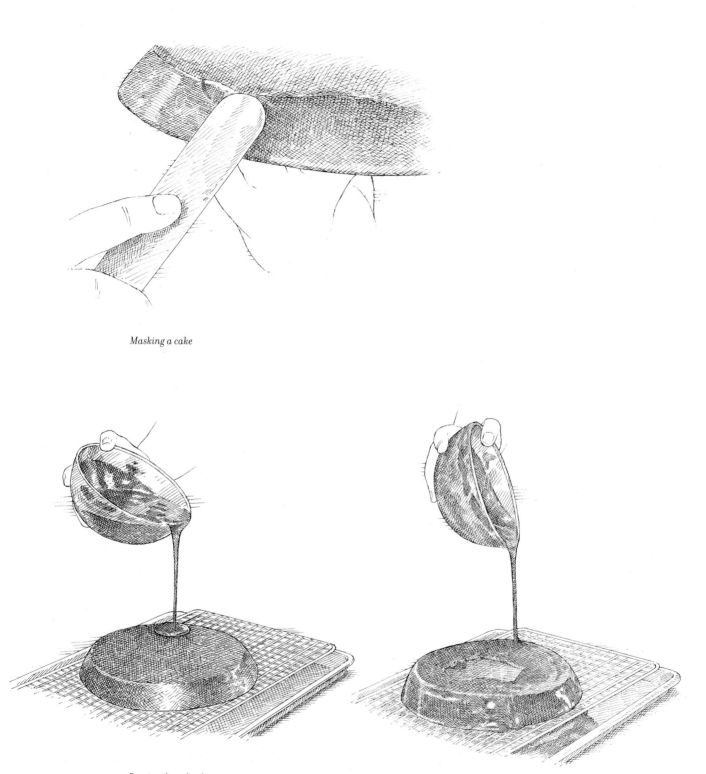

Masking a cake

Pouring the cake glaze

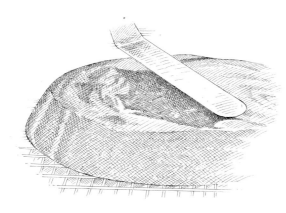

Spreading and finishing the glaze

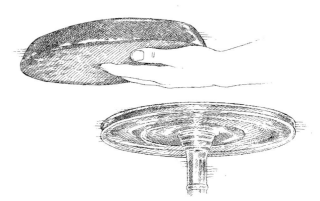

Moving a finished cake

❧ chocolate-dotted cherry torte ❧

This lovely white torte is perfectly delicious without the cherries. But the brandied cherries add a delightful punch that explodes in the mouth, elevating a good cake to greatness.

When I first tasted a dessert like this in a bistro in San Francisco, I was instantly smitten with the idea of a dense white cake flavored with almonds and the tiniest flecks of dark chocolate, like pinpoints that dissolve on the tongue. The fact that it also happens to be easy to make is the proverbial icing on the cake.

serves 12

5 ounces semisweet chocolate, roughly chopped

1 stick (8 tablespoons) unsalted butter, room temperature

¾ cup sugar

3 level tablespoons (1½ ounces) almond paste

3 large eggs, separated

1 tablespoon cornstarch

1 cup cake flour, sifted then measured

1 cup (4 ounces) almond flour (page 19)

1 cup French Grilliotines, brandied cherries, or reconstituted dried cherries (see below)

dark cocoa powder or softly whipped cream, for serving

Position a rack in the middle of the oven and preheat the oven to 300°F.

Butter a 9-inch round cake pan (preferably flared) and line with a parchment circle.

In a food processor, pulse chocolate for 1 minute, being careful not to overprocess. Place in a small bowl. Remove any large pieces of chocolate and reprocess. The finished ground chocolate pieces should be 1/16 to 1/8 inch.

In a mixer fitted with the paddle attachment, cream the butter and ½ cup of the sugar on medium-high speed for 2 minutes. Scrape down the sides of the bowl with a rubber spatula.

With the mixer on high speed, begin adding the almond paste in small pieces, beating until completely smooth, about 2 minutes. Midway through, stop and scrape down the sides of the bowl. Add the egg yolks, one at a time, beating well between additions. The mixture will be pale yellow.

In another bowl with a whisk attachment, begin whipping the egg whites on medium-high speed, increasing the speed until quite frothy. Slowly add the remaining ¼ cup sugar, continuously whipping until the peaks are stiff but not dry. The peaks should be shiny, and the mixture should have a glossy appearance and creamy consistency.

In another mixing bowl, with a fork mix together the cornstarch, sifted cake flour, almond flour, and chocolate.

Alternating in thirds, add the dry ingredients then the whipped egg whites to the creamed butter and sugar mixture, gently folding in each addition by hand with a rubber spatula. The finished batter will be quite thick.

Drain the brandied cherries and evenly scatter on the bottom of the lined cake pan. Gently and evenly spread the batter over the cherries. The pan will be half full.

Bake for 35 to 40 minutes. A cake tester inserted in the center will have a few moist crumbs. Let the cake layer cool in the pan at room temperature for 15 minutes.

To remove from the pan, run a thin-bladed knife around the edges of the cake and invert it onto a serving plate. Peel the parchment and let cool completely. Lightly sprinkle with cocoa powder and serve with loosely whipped cream. Can be stored at room temperature up to 3 days, with cut edges protected.

Gilding the Lily: This simple cake can be dressed up by glazing with 1 recipe Chocolate Butter Glaze (page 214). Follow the instructions for L'Orange (page 52).

{ homemade brandied cherries }

*i*f you can't find French Grilliotines, you can brandy your own dried cherries at home. It takes a few days, so you'll want to plan ahead. Bring a small pan of water to a boil, add 4 ounces tart dried cherries, and remove from heat. Let steep for 10 minutes. Drain and place plumped cherries in a small jar. Pour in enough Kirschwasser or your favorite brandy to cover and seal the jar. Let sit at least 2 to 3 days. Drain liqueur-soaked cherries before using. Save the brandy for other uses.

❧ framboise torte ❧

My goal with the Framboise was to pack as many raspberries as humanly possible into the cake, permeating it with exquisite fragrance without resorting to the crutch of a jam filling. The result is an exceptionally moist, dark chocolate torte drenched with tart raspberry—a combination I never grow tired of.

Berry season in Seattle starts in mid-June and peaks in July. It may be a short season, but it makes up for its length with a vivid intensity. Due to our cool, wet climate, each nodule on the berry grows exceptionally large and juicy. Succulent berries like these are fragile and they don't travel out of state—all the more reason to plan an early summer trip to the Northwest.

Overripe berries are great for baking. The Framboise is a natural for making in a heart-shaped pan for Valentine's Day with frozen raspberries or the imported berries we now have all year round. Serve with lightly whipped cream.

serves 12 to 16

7½ ounces semisweet chocolate, finely chopped

1 stick plus 7 tablespoons unsalted butter, room temperature

7 ounces thawed frozen raspberries, juices reserved or 1¼ cups fresh

½ cup sugar

1 tablespoon Grand Marnier

5 large eggs, separated

¾ cup plus 2 tablespoons sugar (14 tablespoons)

½ cup cake flour, sifted then measured

1 recipe Chocolate Butter Glaze (page 214)

Position a rack in the middle of the oven and preheat the oven to 350°F. Butter a 9-inch round cake pan (preferably flared) and line with a parchment circle.

In a double boiler melt the chocolate over low heat. Remove when nearly melted and continue stirring until completely smooth. Add the softened butter in three parts, stirring until no visible traces of butter remain. (If the butter begins to melt and separate, stop and allow the chocolate more time to cool.) The finished mixture should be glossy and smooth. Set aside to

cool until the mixture is the consistency of softened butter. Briefly return to the double boiler if it begins to thicken too much.

In a food processor purée the raspberries and sugar for 1 minute. Strain through a sieve to remove the seeds. Stir in the Grand Marnier. Set aside.

In a mixer with the whisk attachment, whip the egg yolks with half the sugar at medium-high speed, increasing to high speed until light and tripled in volume, 5 to 6 minutes.

Using a rubber spatula, fold the melted chocolate mixture into the egg mixture. The mixture should be smooth and glossy. Fold in the raspberry purée.

Meanwhile sift the flour and set aside.

Clean and dry the whisk attachment and in another bowl begin whipping the egg whites on medium-high speed, increasing the speed and allowing them to become quite frothy. With the machine on, slowly add the remaining sugar and continue whipping until the peaks are stiff but not dry. The mixture should have a glossy appearance and creamy consistency.

While the egg whites are finishing, fold the sifted flour into the chocolate mixture.

Lighten the chocolate mixture by quickly folding in one-third of the whites, then gently fold in the remaining whites in 2 parts, trying not to overmix and lose the volume. Evenly spread the batter into the prepared pan.

Bake for 45 minutes, until the top appears lighter in color. A cake tester inserted in the center will have a few moist crumbs. Let cake cool at room temperature in the pan for approximately 15 minutes.

To remove from pan, run a thin-bladed knife around the edges of the cake. Invert onto a cardboard cake circle or metal tart pan bottom. Wrap in plastic and chill completely in the refrigerator. (The cake can be wrapped in plastic once cooled and placed in freezer up to a week prior to assembly.)

to finish the torte

Bring the torte to room temperature. Remove the plastic, peel off the parchment paper, and trim any uneven edges.

Have ready the Chocolate Butter Glaze.

Place the torte layer (leaving it on the cardboard cake circle or tart bottom) on a cooling or pouring rack positioned over a rimmed baking sheet. (See pages 54–55.)

Beginning 1½ inches from the edge of the torte, slowly and evenly pour the glaze all around the torte, making sure that the sides are sufficiently covered. Then pour the remaining glaze onto the center.

Working quickly, with a metal offset spatula spread the glaze evenly over the top, letting the excess run down the sides.

Let set at room temperature until glaze is slightly firm, about 5 minutes. Once set, slide an offset spatula under the cardboard circle, rotating the spatula to release any spots where the glaze has stuck to the rack. Carefully lift the torte and, supporting the cake's bottom with your free hand, slide it onto its serving plate. Can be stored at room temperature up to 3 days, with cut edges protected.

VARIATION

To make petit fours like those pictured, the torte may be baked in a 9-by-13-inch sheet pan. Bake 30 to 35 minutes, or until the top becomes light in color and a cake tester has a few moist crumbs. Chill the cake well. Using a warm, dry cutter, carefully cut out the heart shapes. Place on a pouring rack positioned over a rimmed baking sheet. Have ready the Chocolate Butter Glaze (page 214). Pour over the hearts. Let set at room temperature until glaze is slightly firm, about 5 minutes. Once set, slide an offset spatula under the individual petit-fours and move to a serving plate.

·{ the reine }·

The Reine, one of the building blocks of my first pastry shop, has the soft crumb and pure flavor that I adore in a chocolate cake. It is a smart choice for the home baker. Similar in structure to a traditional American cake, it has a creamed-butter-and-sugar base, just enough flour to make it sensible, and eggs only for height. The resulting cake is lighter in texture (and even in color) than the more intense tortes, making it eminently adaptable.

The Reine is lovely without even the butter glaze. You can finish it simply by dusting the top with cocoa, or serving with a scoop of ice cream, a puddle of crème anglaise, a handful of fresh berries, or loosely whipped Caramel Whipped Cream (page 221). You can even tuck the plain cake into a picnic basket. After twenty years, the Reine still reigns!   serves 12 to 16

8 ounces semisweet chocolate, finely chopped

1 stick plus 6 tablespoons unsalted butter, room temperature

1 cup sugar

6 large eggs, separated

1 cup cake flour, sifted then measured

1 cup (4 ounces) almond flour (page 19)

1 recipe Chocolate Butter Glaze (page 214)

Position a rack in the middle of the oven and preheat oven to 300°F.

Butter a 9-inch round cake pan (preferably flared) and line with a parchment circle.

In a double boiler melt the chocolate over low heat. Remove when nearly melted and continue stirring until smooth. Set aside and cool to 90 to 95°F. Return it to the double boiler briefly if it begins to thicken.

In a mixer with the paddle attachment, at medium-high speed cream the butter with ⅓ cup sugar. The mixture should be pale yellow in color and fluffy with no grains of sugar remaining. With the machine running, add the yolks one at a time, scraping the bowl several times between additions, 5 to 6 minutes.

In another bowl, with a fork mix the almond flour and sifted flour. Using a rubber spatula, fold the flour mixture into the butter-yolk mixture. Fold in the melted chocolate. The mixture should be smooth and glossy.

In another mixer bowl, with a clean whisk attachment begin whipping the egg whites on medium-high speed, increasing the speed and beating until quite frothy. Slowly add the remaining sugar and continue whipping until the peaks are stiff but not dry. The peaks should be shiny, and the mixture should look glossy with a creamy consistency.   (continued)

Lighten the chocolate mixture by quickly folding in a third of the whites, then gently fold in the remaining whites in 2 parts, trying not to overmix and lose the volume. Spread the batter evenly in the prepared pan.

Bake for 60 minutes, until the top appears lighter in color. A cake tester inserted in the center will have a few moist crumbs. Let the cake cool in the pan at room temperature for approximately 15 minutes.

To remove from the pan, run a thin-bladed knife along the edges and invert onto a cardboard cake circle or metal tart pan bottom. Wrap in plastic and chill completely. (The torte can be frozen up to a week prior to assembly.)

to finish the torte

Have ready the Chocolate Butter Glaze.

Bring the torte to room temperature, unwrap it, and remove the parchment paper. Trim any uneven edges.

Place the torte (leaving it on the cardboard cake circle or tart bottom) on a cooling or pouring rack positioned over a rimmed baking sheet.

Beginning 1½ inches from the edge of the torte, slowly and evenly pour the glaze all around the torte layer, making sure that the sides are sufficiently covered. Then pour the remaining glaze onto the center of the torte.

Working quickly, with a metal offset spatula spread the glaze evenly over the top, letting the excess run down the sides.

Let set at room temperature until glaze is slightly firm, about 5 minutes. Once set, slide an offset spatula under the cardboard circle, rotating the spatula to release any spots where the glaze has stuck to the rack. Carefully lift the torte and, supporting the cake's bottom with your free hand, slide it onto its serving plate. Can be stored at room temperature up to 3 days, with cut edges protected.

whipping egg whites

Room-temperature whites are easier to beat than cold ones. It's most important to work with a totally clean bowl and whisk since the slightest trace of fat will inhibit their rising. Just to be safe, always wipe bowls clean with a towel before beginning.

In a heavy-duty mixer, with the balloon whisk start beating egg whites at medium speed until white and frothy. When there is no longer a pool of liquid on the bottom and the foam starts mounting the sides, start slowly sprinkling in the sugar, beating continuously. When all of the sugar has been added, turn the speed up to high. For the soft peaks that most batters call for, whites are done when very glossy and they ribbon off the whisk when lifted. Soft peaks should mound in the bowl with peak tops that flop. Beating some sugar into the whites helps stabilize and prevent overbeating. Nonetheless, always treat your whipped egg whites like the delicate creatures that they are. They start deflating immediately.

⊹} chocolate apricot pecan torte {⊹

With its juicy bits of brandied fruit and nuts, this dense torte falls somewhere between a holiday fruitcake and a torte. I like to serve it in October to start everyone dreaming about the indulgences to come during the winter holiday season. It is a great favorite of apricot lovers all year round. Since the ganache glaze needs time to thicken to spreading consistency, start the glaze the day before.   serves 12 to 16

1 recipe Dark Chocolate Ganache Glaze (page 215)

3 ounces dried apricots, finely chopped in food processor or by hand into ⅛-inch pieces

¼ cup plus 2 tablespoons brandy

10 ounces semisweet chocolate, finely chopped

1 stick plus 2 tablespoons unsalted butter, room temperature

4 large eggs, separated

1 cup plus 2 tablespoons sugar (18 tablespoons)

½ cup plus 1 tablespoon cake flour, sifted then measured

1⅔ cups (5 ounces) pecans, toasted and finely ground

1 cup (3 ounces) pecans, toasted and finely chopped

2–3 tablespoons Dutch-processed cocoa powder

Make Dark-Chocolate Ganache Glaze 8 to 12 hours before finishing the cake. You will not be pouring this glaze, but using it to frost the torte. Follow these instructions for using the glaze as a frosting/icing: When the chocolate and cream are combined and smooth, cover with plastic wrap touching the surface to prevent a skin from forming and set aside. Let the ganache cool without stirring. Let it set up at room temperature for 8 to 12 hours or overnight. When the ganache is the consistency of soft butter, it is ready to use.

To speed things up, you may let sit at room temperature, uncovered, about 4 hours. Gently fold with a spatula every 20 to 30 minutes to thicken.

Soak the chopped apricots in the brandy for 1 hour.

Position a rack in the middle of the oven and preheat the oven to 325°F. Butter a 9-inch round cake pan (preferably flared) and line with parchment paper.

In a double boiler melt the chocolate over low heat. Remove when nearly melted and continue stirring until completely smooth. Add the softened butter in 3 parts, stirring until no visible traces of butter remain. (If the butter begins to melt and separate, stop and allow the chocolate more time to cool.) The finished mixture should be glossy and smooth. Set aside to cool until the mixture is the consistency of softened butter. Briefly return to the double boiler if it begins to thicken too much.

(continued)

In a mixer with the whisk attachment, whip the egg yolks with 12 tablespoons sugar at medium-high speed, increasing to high speed until light and tripled in volume (about 5 to 6 minutes). Set aside.

Clean the whisk, and in another clean bowl begin whipping the egg whites on medium-high speed, increasing the speed until quite frothy. Slowly add the remaining sugar and continue whipping, increasing the speed to high until the peaks are stiff but not dry. The whites should be glossy with a creamy consistency.

Combine the sifted cake flour and the 1⅔ cups ground pecans. Gently fold into the yolk mixture. Then fold the chocolate and butter mixture into the same bowl. Fold in the apricots and brandy.

Lighten the chocolate mixture by quickly folding in a third of the whites. Then gently fold in the remaining whites in 2 parts, trying not to overmix and lose the volume.

Evenly spread the batter into the prepared pan.

Bake for 60 to 65 minutes, until the top appears lighter in color and a tester inserted in the center comes out clean. Set aside to cool in the pan at room temperature about 10 minutes.

To remove from the pan, run a thin-bladed knife along the edges and invert onto a cardboard cake circle or metal tart bottom. Cool completely. The cooled torte can be wrapped in plastic and frozen up to a week.

to finish the torte

Unwrap the torte layer and trim any uneven edges if necessary. Remove the parchment paper circle.

Using a metal spatula, thinly frost the sides of the torte and then the top with the Dark-Chocolate Ganache Glaze. It is important to work quickly, as any time you move or stir the ganache, it will stiffen. With the palms of your hands, press the chopped pecans onto the sides of the cake.

To decorate, cut out ten 9-by-½-inch strips of parchment paper. Make a checkerboard pattern by arranging 5 strips evenly across the top of the cake. Then arrange the remaining strips evenly across the top of the cake, crossing the other strips at a 90-degree angle. With a fine-mesh sieve, dust the top of the torte with cocoa powder. Carefully lift the parchment strips and discard. Transfer to a serving plate. Can be stored at room temperature up to 3 days, with cut edges protected.

Gilding the Lily: You can pipe a shell border along the top edge of the torte with the remaining ganache. Fill a pastry bag fitted with a #18 tip and pipe a shell border.

⁛{ chocolate single-malt scotch torte }⁛

A great single-malt Scotch behaves like Cognac when paired with chocolate. It allows the chocolate flavors to bloom while adding its own distinctive perfume. Scotch also keeps the cake moist, making this torte a good keeper. Serve thin slices with the same Scotch you used for baking and consider yourself rewarded for being a grown-up! This elegant Scotch and chocolate combination is a perfect ending to fall and winter dinners. serves 12 to 16

8½ ounces semisweet chocolate, finely chopped

1 stick plus 2 tablespoons unsalted butter, room temperature

4 large eggs, separated

⅔ cup sugar

3 tablespoons single-malt Scotch

½ cup cake flour, sifted then measured

1 cup (4 ounces) almond flour (page 19)

1 recipe Chocolate Butter Glaze (page 214)

Position a rack in the middle of the oven and preheat the oven to 325°F. Butter a 9-inch round cake pan (preferably flared) and line with a parchment circle.

In a double boiler melt the chocolate over low heat. Remove when nearly melted and continue stirring until completely smooth. Add the softened butter in 3 parts, stirring until no visible traces of butter remain. (If the butter begins to melt and separate, stop and allow the chocolate more time to cool.) The finished mixture should be glossy and smooth. Set aside to cool until the mixture is the consistency of softened butter. Briefly return to the double boiler if the mixture begins to thicken too much.

In a mixer fitted with the whisk attachment, whip the egg yolks with ⅓ cup sugar at medium-high speed, increasing to high speed until light and tripled in volume, 5 to 6 minutes.

Remove the mixing bowl and, using a rubber spatula, fold the melted chocolate mixture into the egg mixture. Then fold in the Scotch. The mixture should be smooth and glossy.

Meanwhile with a fork blend together the sifted flour and the almond flour. Set aside.

Clean the whisk and in another clean bowl begin whipping the egg whites on medium-high speed, increasing the speed and allowing them to become quite frothy. Slowly add the remaining sugar and continue whipping until the peaks are stiff but not dry. The mixture should have a glossy appearance and creamy consistency.

While the egg whites are finishing, fold the flours into the chocolate mixture.

Lighten the chocolate mixture by quickly folding in one-third of the whites, then gently fold in the remaining whites in 2 parts, trying not to overmix and lose the volume. Evenly spread the batter into the prepared pan. It will be two-thirds full.

Place the torte in the oven and lower the temperature to 300°F. Bake for 35 to 40 minutes, until the top appears lighter in color. A cake tester inserted in the center will have a few moist crumbs. Cool the cake in the pan at room temperature for 15 minutes.

To remove from the pan, run a thin-bladed knife around the edges of the cake, turning the layer out onto a tart bottom or 9-inch cardboard cake circle. Let cool completely at room temperature and peel off the parchment if finishing. (The layer can be wrapped in plastic with the parchment attached, cooled, and placed in freezer up to a week prior to assembly.)

to finish the torte

Bring the torte to room temperature, unwrap it, remove parchment paper. Trim uneven edges.

Have ready the Chocolate Butter Glaze.

Place the layer (leaving it on the cardboard cake circle or tart bottom) on a cooling or pouring rack positioned over a rimmed baking sheet. (See pages 54–55.)

Beginning 1½ inches from the edge of the torte, slowly and evenly pour the glaze all around the torte layer, making sure that the sides are sufficiently covered. Then pour the remaining glaze onto the center of the torte.

Working quickly, with a metal offset spatula spread the glaze evenly over the top, letting the excess run down the sides.

Let set at room temperature until glaze is slightly firm, about 5 minutes. Once set, slide an offset spatula under the cardboard circle, rotating the spatula to release any spots where the glaze has stuck to the rack. Carefully lift the torte and, supporting the cake's bottom with your free hand, slide it onto its serving plate. Can be stored at room temperature up to 3 days, with cut edges protected.

❖{ pavé josephine }❖

Josephine, my first cooking teacher, always said that "one had to be a perfectionist to master desserts." I named this dense chocolate torte for her because it captures the essence of French style and taste. Made with three simple ingredients—chocolate, butter, and eggs—it is pure luxury. Pavé is a wonderful choice for the inexperienced baker and over-the-top chocoholic. But you must take Josephine's advice and follow the directions to the letter! For a quick, uncomplicated dessert, the Pavé Josephine need not be glazed.

serves 16

1¼ pounds semisweet chocolate, finely chopped

½ pound (2 sticks) unsalted butter, room temperature

6 large eggs, room temperature

1 recipe Chocolate Butter Glaze (page 214) (optional)

Position a rack in the middle of the oven and preheat the oven to 300°F. Butter a 9-inch round cake pan and line the bottom with a parchment paper circle.

In a double boiler melt the chocolate over low heat. Remove when nearly melted and continue stirring until completely smooth. Add the softened butter in 3 parts, stirring until no visible traces of butter remain. (If the butter begins to melt and separate, stop and allow the chocolate more time to cool.) The finished mixture should be glossy and smooth. Set aside to cool until the mixture is the consistency of softened butter. Briefly return to the double boiler if it begins to thicken too much.

In a mixer fitted with the whisk attachment, whip the eggs at medium-high speed, increasing to high speed until light and tripled in volume, 5 to 6 minutes.

Fold the eggs into the chocolate mixture and pour into the prepared pan.

Place the cake pan on a heavy-duty rimmed baking sheet, and put in the preheated oven. Pour about ½ inch of simmering water into the baking sheet, making a bain-marie. Bake for 30 to 35 minutes, until the top looks dull and the center is shiny but set. When you shake the cake pan, the cake should jiggle slightly.

Cool the cake in the pan at room temperature for 1 to 2 hours. To remove from the pan, run a thin-bladed knife around the edges and invert onto a cardboard cake circle or tart bottom, leaving the parchment in place. Wrap with plastic wrap and chill.

to finish the torte

Remove from the refrigerator, unwrap, and peel off the parchment. Place the cake on a cooling or pouring rack positioned over a rimmed baking sheet. Let warm to room temperature before glazing.

(continued)

Have ready the Chocolate Butter Glaze.

Beginning 1½ inches from the edge of the torte, slowly and evenly pour the glaze all around the torte, making sure that the sides are sufficiently covered (see page 54–55). Then pour the remaining glaze onto the center of the torte.

Working quickly, with a metal offset spatula spread the glaze evenly over the top, letting the excess run down the sides.

Let set at room temperature until glaze is slightly firm, about 5 minutes. Once set, slide an offset spatula under the cardboard circle, rotating the spatula to release any spots where the glaze has stuck to the rack. Carefully lift the torte and, supporting the cake's bottom with your free hand, slide it onto its serving plate. Can be stored at room temperature up to 3 days, with cut edges protected.

the torte test

*m*y tortes are moist, dense, single-layer cakes made without artificial leaveners or much flour. Removing them from the oven at the exact right moment makes all the difference. Since there is a five-minute window when a torte begins to dry out, you want to start checking delicate tortes five minutes before the end of the baking time in the recipe. Pierce with a toothpick about 2 inches from the edge, since a cake bakes from the outside edges to the center. If it comes out clean, test the center. The center (and the cake) will be done when moist crumbs cling to the toothpick. This should take no longer than five minutes. If a torte is removed too soon the center may collapse as it cools because the batter is still partially raw. And a torte cooked too long will never be as moist as it was meant to be.

❧ chocolate espresso torte ❧

Here in Seattle, where we take our coffee and chocolate very seriously, I created the ultimate, melt-in-your-mouth custard cake to celebrate this sensational duo. It attains maximum smoothness by baking in a very slow oven and a pampering water bath. If you've ever ordered this sophisticated dessert from our catalog, you know that a little sliver goes a long, long way. It is as intensely rich as an espresso truffle.

serves 16

1 pound semisweet chocolate, finely chopped

¾ pound (3 sticks) unsalted butter, room temperature

½ cup freshly brewed lukewarm espresso, or ½ cup lukewarm double-strength coffee plus 1½ teaspoons instant espresso powder

¾ cup sugar

8 large eggs, room temperature

1 recipe Chocolate Butter Glaze (page 214)

Position a rack in the middle of the oven and preheat the oven to 300°F. Butter a 9-inch round cake pan and line with a parchment circle.

In a double boiler melt the chocolate over low heat. Remove when nearly melted and continue stirring until completely smooth. Add the softened butter in 3 parts, stirring until no visible traces of butter remain. (If the butter begins to melt and separate, stop and allow the chocolate more time to cool.) The finished mixture should be glossy and smooth. Set aside to cool until the mixture is the consistency of softened butter. Briefly return to the double boiler if it begins to thicken too much.

Place the chocolate-and-butter mixture in the bowl of an electric mixer. Using the paddle attachment, begin mixing the chocolate and butter at low speed, slowly pouring in the tepid espresso or coffee mixture. Scrape down the sides of the bowl with a rubber spatula several times to ensure thorough mixing.

With the machine running on low slowly add the sugar.

In a small bowl gently whisk the eggs together just to blend. With the machine still on low speed, add the eggs in a thin, steady stream, being careful not to incorporate too much air. Stop and scrape down the sides of the bowl with a rubber spatula several times to ensure thorough mixing. The mixture should be as thick as melted chocolate, and perfectly smooth and glossy.

Pour into the prepared pan, smoothing the top. Place the pan on a rimmed heavy-duty baking sheet, and place in the oven. Pour approximately ½ inch of simmering water into the baking sheet for a bain-marie. Bake for 50 to 60 minutes, until the top looks dull and the center is shiny but set. When you shake the pan, the cake should slightly jiggle. Some blistering may appear on top of the cake. *(continued)*

Let the cake cool in the pan for about 30 minutes. Then loosely cover and refrigerate 2 to 4 hours. To remove the cake from the pan, run a thin-bladed knife around the edges to loosen and invert onto a cardboard cake circle or tart bottom.

to finish the torte

Bring the torte to room temperature, unwrap it, and remove parchment paper.

Have ready the Chocolate Butter Glaze.

Place the torte on a cooling or pouring rack positioned over a rimmed baking sheet. (See pages 54–55.)

Beginning 1½ inches from the edge of the torte, slowly and evenly pour the glaze all around the torte, making sure that the sides are sufficiently covered. Then pour the remaining glaze onto the center of the torte.

Working quickly, with a metal offset spatula spread the glaze evenly over the top, letting the excess run down the sides.

Let set at room temperature until the glaze is slightly firm, about 5 minutes. Once set, slide an offset spatula under the cardboard circle, rotating the spatula to release any spots where the glaze has stuck to the rack. Carefully lift the torte and, supporting the cake's bottom with your free hand, slide it onto its serving plate. Can be stored at room temperature up to 3 days, with cut edges protected.

❧{ chocolate cabernet torte }❧

When my son, Dylan, attended culinary school in California's wine country, my husband, Peter, and I had the perfect excuse to visit the wineries and really savor the wines. After some serious tasting it occurred to me that fruity cabernet hit just the right cherry notes to marry well with my favorite ingredient.

Once I came up with the technique of carefully reducing cabernet down to its robust essence, the next step was to capture that fruitiness in this fabulously rich flourless torte. I like to serve very thin slices of this confection-style cake after a particularly rich meal.

I believe in saving your best red wines for drinking. For baking, a modestly priced, trusted bottle is fine. You also can substitute 3 tablespoons of your favorite liqueur for the wine essence and create your own extravagant torte.

serves 12 to 16

1½ cups cabernet or cabernet-merlot-blend wine

3 tablespoons plus ¼ cup sugar

1 pound bittersweet chocolate (70% cacao), finely chopped

1 cup heavy cream

6 large eggs

dark cocoa powder for decoration

Crème Anglaise (page 173) for serving

Position a rack in the middle of the oven and preheat the oven to 325°F. Butter a 9-inch round cake pan (preferably flared) and line with a parchment circle.

In a small saucepan over medium-high heat, combine the cabernet and 3 tablespoons of sugar. Bring to a simmer and cook until reduced to 3 tablespoons, about 20 to 25 minutes. Stay nearby and keep adjusting the heat downward to maintain the lowest simmer. You want to avoid any boiling since the wine can evaporate and scorch, throwing the flavor off, especially in the last 5 to 10 minutes. Set aside to cool.

In a double boiler melt the chocolate over low heat. Remove when nearly melted and continue stirring until smooth. Return it to the double boiler only briefly if it begins to thicken too much.

Whip cream to soft peaks and set aside in the refrigerator.

In the bowl of the electric mixer, combine the whole eggs with the remaining ¼ cup sugar and the cooled cabernet syrup. Pour

tortes, with and without flour

1 inch water into a medium skillet and bring to a simmer. Place the mixing bowl in the pan of water, stirring with a rubber spatula until the mixture is warm, about 110°F.

Wipe off the bottom and place the mixing bowl on the mixer fitted with a whisk attachment. Beat at medium-high speed, increasing to high speed until the egg mixture is pale in color, tripled in volume, and holds soft peaks, 5 to 6 minutes.

Remove the bowl from the stand. Using a rubber spatula, gently fold in the melted chocolate. The mixture will deflate to about half its original volume. Fold the chilled whipped cream into the chocolate mixture until no visible traces of cream remain.

Pour the batter into the pan and bake for 40 minutes, or until a cake tester inserted in the center comes out clean. The center should just be set. Let cool in pan for 30 minutes.

To remove from the pan, run a thin-bladed knife around the edge of the cake. Turn the cake out onto a serving plate or 9-inch cardboard cake circle and cool completely before removing the parchment paper.

To serve, remove the parchment. Using a small sieve, dust the top of the torte with cocoa powder. Pour the Creme Anglais (allow 3 to 4 tablespoons per serving) onto a dessert plate or bowl, and serve a piece of the torte atop it.

Can be stored at room temperature up to 3 days, with cut edges protected.

{ elegant tarts }

❊⟩ dark-chocolate caramel nut tart ⟨❊

Inspired by the tin roof sundae, the classic cold treat of vanilla ice cream, chocolate and caramel sauces, and roasted peanuts, this three-part tart blends chocolate, nuts, and caramel into one elegant dessert. The crust is an easy, all-nut pastry that you just press into the pan, and the finished tart can be kept in the refrigerator for several days without losing flavor. For the autumn holidays you can also fill the crust with fresh cranberries boiled with a little sugar or pumpkin custard.

serves 12

one 9-inch Walnut Tart Crust, baked and cooled (page 226)

caramel sauce

¾ cup sugar

¾ cup water

½ cup heavy cream, warmed

chocolate ganache topping

7 ounces heavy cream

8 ounces semisweet chocolate, finely chopped

Have ready the Walnut Tart Crust.

to make the caramel sauce

In a heavy medium saucepan combine the sugar and water. Cook over medium heat, without stirring, until the liquid is clear and the sugar dissolved, 5 minutes. Raise the heat to medium-high and bring the mixture to a boil, washing down the sides of the pan with a wet pastry brush if crystals form. Continue boiling until the sugar turns golden brown, 10 to 15 minutes.

Remove from the heat. Averting your face to avoid splatters, slowly and carefully pour in the warm cream. When the bubbling subsides, stir until well combined. Pour a spoonful onto a saucer to test the consistency. A spoon run through the caramel should briefly hold a channel.

If too thin, return to heat and cook a few minutes longer. Pour into the baked crust.

to make the chocolate ganache

In a small pot, heat the cream over medium-high heat until it begins to simmer. Remove from the heat and stir in the chocolate until smooth. Let cool until about 80–85°F. Slowly pour over the cooled caramel layer, spreading evenly to the edges. Let set at room temperature. Serve and store at room temperature. Can be kept for up to 4 days.

VARIATION

For a quick cranberry filling, in a saucepan over medium heat cook together 1 (12-ounce) bag of fresh cranberries with 1 cup sugar, ½ cup red currant jelly, and ½ cup water just until the berries pop. Let cool and spoon into baked, cooled tart shell. Serve with White Chocolate Whipped Cream (page 219).

⁂⟩ pure chocolate tart ⟨⁂

Gently baking the puddinglike filling in this classic French pastry makes
all the difference. It intensifies the chocolate, making the contrast between
crisp cookie crust and smooth, silky filling completely delectable. An easy
tart such as this should be high on your list of emergency desserts for
visiting chocoholics.   serves 12

3 large egg yolks

1 cup plus 2 tablespoons heavy
cream

12 ounces semisweet chocolate,
finely chopped

1 tablespoon pure vanilla extract

one 9-inch Sugar Tart Crust or
twelve 3-inch tart shells, baked and
cooled (page 224)

Preheat the oven to 300°F.

In a mixing bowl, lightly whisk together
the egg yolks and set aside.

In a small saucepan, heat the cream over
medium-high heat until it begins to boil.
Remove from the heat. Stir in the chocolate until smooth, using a rubber spatula.

Pour about one-third of the chocolate
mixture into the yolks and quickly stir
with the spatula. Pour in the remaining
chocolate and stir until smooth. Stir in the
vanilla.

Pour into the baked tart shell, smoothing
the top with a metal spatula. Place on a
baking sheet. Bake for 15 minutes, until
the surface is glossy and the edges slightly
puffed. Do not worry about small air
bubbles forming around the edges.

Let cool to room temperature before
serving. Store in the refrigerator.

⋅⋅{ key lime white-chocolate tart }⋅⋅

White chocolate enriches a classic lime curd, elevating it to an even more sensuous smoothness. The contrast between crisp, dark chocolate crust and tart-sweet lime custard is fantastic. Serve with a bowl of lightly whipped cream for the perfect finishing touch.

serves 12

8 large egg yolks

1 cup sugar

⅔ cup key lime juice, fresh or bottled

4 ounces white chocolate, finely chopped

1 stick (8 tablespoons) unsalted butter, room temperature, cut into 16 pieces

one 9-inch Chocolate Wafer Tart Crust or twelve 3-inch tart shells, baked and cooled (page 222)

Place the egg yolks and sugar in a heavy medium saucepan and immediately whisk until smooth. Add the key lime juice and whisk again.

Place over low heat. Cook, stirring constantly with a heat-resistant spatula, until the mixture thickens. When you notice the first bubble of a boil, immediately remove from the heat. Add the finely chopped white chocolate. Stir until smooth. Add the butter, a piece at a time, stirring until completely smooth and incorporated.

Pour into the baked tart shell, smoothing the surface. Chill about 4 hours to set. Bring back to room temperature to serve. Store in the refrigerator.

⋇{ milk-chocolate mocha tart }⋇

Dark-roasted coffee and a cocoa crust accentuate the deeper nuances of the milk chocolate. The subtle scent of lemon provides a bright fresh finish.

serves 12

⅓ cup dark-roast coffee beans, preferably Sumatra

17 ounces dark milk chocolate (42–46% cacao) or 14 ounces light milk chocolate plus 3 ounces semisweet chocolate, finely chopped

1½ cups heavy cream

2 strips lemon peel, cut with a vegetable peeler, about 1 x 3 inches

one 9-inch Chocolate Wafer Tart Crust or twelve 3-inch tart shells, baked and cooled (page 222)

Place the coffee beans in a small plastic ziplock bag. Roll and bash several times with a rolling pin to crack the beans into large pieces. Set aside.

In a double boiler melt the chocolate over low heat. Remove when nearly melted and stir until smooth. Cool slightly.

Place the cream, crushed coffee beans, and lemon peel in a saucepan. Cook over medium-high heat until the mixture just begins to boil. Remove from the heat and let steep for 5 minutes.

Pour the cream through a fine-mesh sieve into the melted chocolate, stirring gently with a rubber spatula. Pour the filling into the prebaked tart shell(s), smoothing the top if necessary. Place in the refrigerator to set for about 4 hours.

Remove from the refrigerator about 2 hours before serving. Do not be concerned if some beads of moisture appear on the surface. They will disappear as the tart warms to room temperature. Milk-Chocolate Mocha Tart can be stored in the refrigerator for 3 days.

White-Chocolate Crème Citron Tart (opposite, top)
Milk-Chocolate Mocha Tart (opposite, below)

❖{ white-chocolate crème citron tart }❖

If it's true that the world's dessert lovers can be split into two camps—the lemon lovers and the chocolate people—then this refreshing twist on lemon curd is guaranteed to elicit smiles on both sides. I experimented with the amount of butter in a typical curd, substituting white chocolate for added richness and that all-important chocolate flavor. All that's needed is lightly whipped cream for a truly sublime dessert experience.   serves 12

8 large egg yolks

1 cup sugar

⅔ cup fresh lemon juice

4 ounces white chocolate, finely chopped

1 stick (8 tablespoons) unsalted butter, room temperature, cut into 16 pieces

one 9-inch Sugar Tart Crust or twelve 3-inch tart shells, baked and cooled (page 224)

Place the egg yolks and sugar in a heavy medium saucepan. Immediately whisk together until smooth. Add the lemon juice and whisk again.

Place saucepan over low heat. Cook the egg yolk mixture, stirring constantly with a heat-resistant spatula, until the mixture thickens and you notice the first bubble of a boil. Immediately remove from the heat. Add the white chocolate and stir until smooth. Add the butter, a piece at a time, stirring until completely incorporated.

Pour into the baked tart shell and chill to set, about 4 hours. Store in the refrigerator for up to 2 days. Bring back to room temperature to serve.

chocolate caramel nut tart

Envision a low, one-inch tart shell baked to a golden brown and then piled high with a glistening array of chunky, whole nuts coated in caramel. Life doesn't get much better for the caramel and nut obsessed. If you need to shave off a few minutes, my dessert sauces are available over the Internet and in the catalog—just order, heat, and pour. During the holidays I like to make this festive tart with pecans only, and with my Caramel Sauce.   serves 12–16

3 cups mixed nuts such as pecans, walnuts, filberts, macadamias, and almonds

1½ cups Chocolate Caramel Sauce (page 178)

one 9-inch Sugar Tart Crust or twelve to sixteen 3-inch tart shells, baked and cooled (page 224)

Preheat the oven to 300°F. Spread the nuts, one type at a time, on a baking sheet and toast in the oven for 5 to 10 minutes, or until their fragrance is released. Each kind of nut should be toasted separately since they cook at different rates. Toss the toasted nuts together in a mixing bowl and set aside.

Warm the Chocolate Caramel Sauce over a pan of simmering water or in a double boiler. Pour over the nuts, tossing with a wooden spoon or rubber spatula to coat evenly.

Mound the caramel-coated nut mixture into the baked tart shell(s). The tart can be stored at room temperature for 3 days.

❧ bitter chocolate almond tart ❧

A cross between a cake and a tart, this sophisticated French pastry is a soufflèed puff of almond cake with a scattering of dark chocolate dots for accent. With its pure, light almond taste, this beauty is a great choice for a summer night on the patio. It can sit out for hours and is delightful with some sliced strawberries or a handful of fresh raspberries. **serves 12**

one 9-inch Sugar Tart Crust (page 224), chilled and unbaked

2 ounces bittersweet chocolate (preferably 70% cacao), finely chopped

2 large eggs, separated, room temperature

½ cup sugar

¾ cup almond flour (page 19)

3 tablespoons milk

2 tablespoons sliced almonds for decoration

Position a rack in the middle of the oven and preheat the oven to 325°F.

Place the unbaked tart shell on a baking sheet and put in the oven. Bake for 10 to 15 minutes, until lightly golden and partially cooked. Set aside to cool. Reduce the oven temperature to 300°F.

In a food processor, pulse the chocolate until ground to pieces no larger than $\frac{1}{16}$ to $\frac{1}{8}$ inch. Set aside.

In a bowl stir together the egg yolks, half of the sugar, the almond flour, and the milk. Place over simmering water or in a double boiler. Cook, stirring constantly, until the mixture is warm to the touch and the sugar has dissolved. Remove from the heat and set aside.

By hand or using a mixer, whip the egg whites until quite frothy. Slowly add the remaining sugar, continuously whipping until the peaks are stiff and glossy.

With a rubber spatula fold one-third of the whipped egg whites into the almond mixture. Fold in the ground chocolate. Then continue folding the remaining whites in 2 or 3 parts. Pour into the partially baked tart shell. Sprinkle with the sliced almonds or see instructions for Gilding the Lily.

Place on a baking sheet and slide into the oven. Bake at 300°F for 25 to 30 minutes, until the top is puffy and golden brown. Let cool on a rack. Store tightly wrapped for 2 to 3 days.

Gilding the Lily: This simple tart can be decorated to look like the photograph (page 86). Omit sprinkling with sliced almonds before baking. Lightly toast 4 ounces sliced almonds (page 19). After the tart has baked, arrange the most perfect toasted almonds in concentric circles on the top.

white-chocolate raspberry tart

In this easy spin on a Linzer torte, two layers of tart raspberries—a quick homemade jam and a row of bright, fresh berries—contrast with a smooth layer of rich white chocolate. With its sturdy nut crust and bright red berries, this festive tart is a natural to take along on summer picnics and potlucks.

serves 12

one 9-inch Walnut Tart Crust, baked and cooled (page 226)

½ recipe Raspberry Filling from Marguerite Torte variation (page 100)

½ cup heavy cream

8 ounces white chocolate, finely chopped

2 pints fresh raspberries, picked clean

Remove the sides of the tart pan and place the crust on a serving plate. Thinly and evenly spread the Raspberry Filling over the base of the tart shell.

In a saucepan, heat the cream on medium-high heat until it begins to simmer. Immediately remove from the heat. With a rubber spatula stir in the chopped chocolate until smooth. Let cool until about 80–85°F. Slowly pour over the Raspberry Filling in the tart shell, up to the rim, spreading evenly to the edges. Let set in the refrigerator about 4 hours.

When the tart is chilled, arrange fresh raspberries, pointy side up, in a circular pattern over the white chocolate filling.

Best served and eaten the day it is made.

VARIATION

A 9-inch square tart pan can be used to make a square tart like the one in the photograph.

✷❧ florentine tart ❧✷

During the winter holidays I like to pull out all the stops. This two-crusted extravaganza has it all—luscious caramel sauce, roasted macadamia nuts, and two layers of dark-chocolate crust to showcase and protect all that rich, oozing filling. When we baked the Florentine for this book, we tasted it with scoops of homemade White Chocolate Coconut Ice Cream (page 149). The combination was divine!

serves 16 to 18

1 recipe Chocolate Wafer Tart Crust dough (page 222), chilled

1⅓ cups sugar

¼ teaspoon cream of tartar

1 cup heavy cream

1¾ cups (8 ounces) macadamia nuts, toasted

½ stick (4 tablespoons) unsalted butter, room temperature

to make the filling

In a heavy medium saucepan, stir together 1 cup water, the sugar, and the cream of tartar. Cover and place over medium heat. Bring to a boil and cook, covered, for 10 minutes.

Remove the cover and continue cooking until the mixture is a light caramel color, 320°F. Reduce the heat to low, and slowly pour in the cream in a thin steady stream, stirring constantly with a wooden spoon until smooth. Add the macadamia nuts and continue stirring until the mixture reaches softball stage (238–242°F) on a candy thermometer. Remove from the heat, and stir in the softened butter.

Pour into a bowl and let cool to room temperature. Then cover with plastic wrap and set aside. The filling can be made well in advance.

to finish the tart

Position a rack in the middle of the oven and preheat the oven to 350°F. Lightly butter a 9-inch fluted tart pan with removable bottom.

Remove the chilled dough from the refrigerator. Divide in half. Rewrap and return one half to the refrigerator. Let the first half warm on the counter for about 10 minutes, until pliable but still cool to the touch.

On a lightly floured board, gently knead the dough a few times. Pat into a ball, then flatten into a 5-inch round disk with the palms of your hands. With a floured rolling pin, begin rolling from the center out, lifting and turning until an 11½-inch circle, about ⅛ inch thick, is formed. Keep dusting the board and pin with all-purpose flour as needed.

Gently lift and roll the dough onto the rolling pin, brushing off any excess flour with a pastry brush. Place the dough in the buttered tart pan and unroll, taking care not to roll the pin along the top of the pan.

Press the dough evenly over the bottom and around the edges of the tart pan, so the sides are even and thick. (Cracks can be repaired by lightly moistening the broken edges with a few drops of water and patching with small scraps of dough.)

Gently spoon all the filling into the tart shell and set aside.

Remove the remaining dough from the refrigerator and follow the same procedure for rolling out the top crust. The top should be slightly smaller in size.

With a pastry brush and water lightly moisten the top edges of the filled tart shell.

Gently roll and lift the top crust and place over the nut filling to completely cover. Lightly pinch the edges together to seal. Using a sharp paring knife, trim the excess tart dough along the edges. Chill completely.

Place on a parchment-lined baking sheet, and slide into the oven. Bake for 25 to 30 minutes, until the top crust is dry and firm. Let cool on a rack. Store at room temperature as long as 4 days.

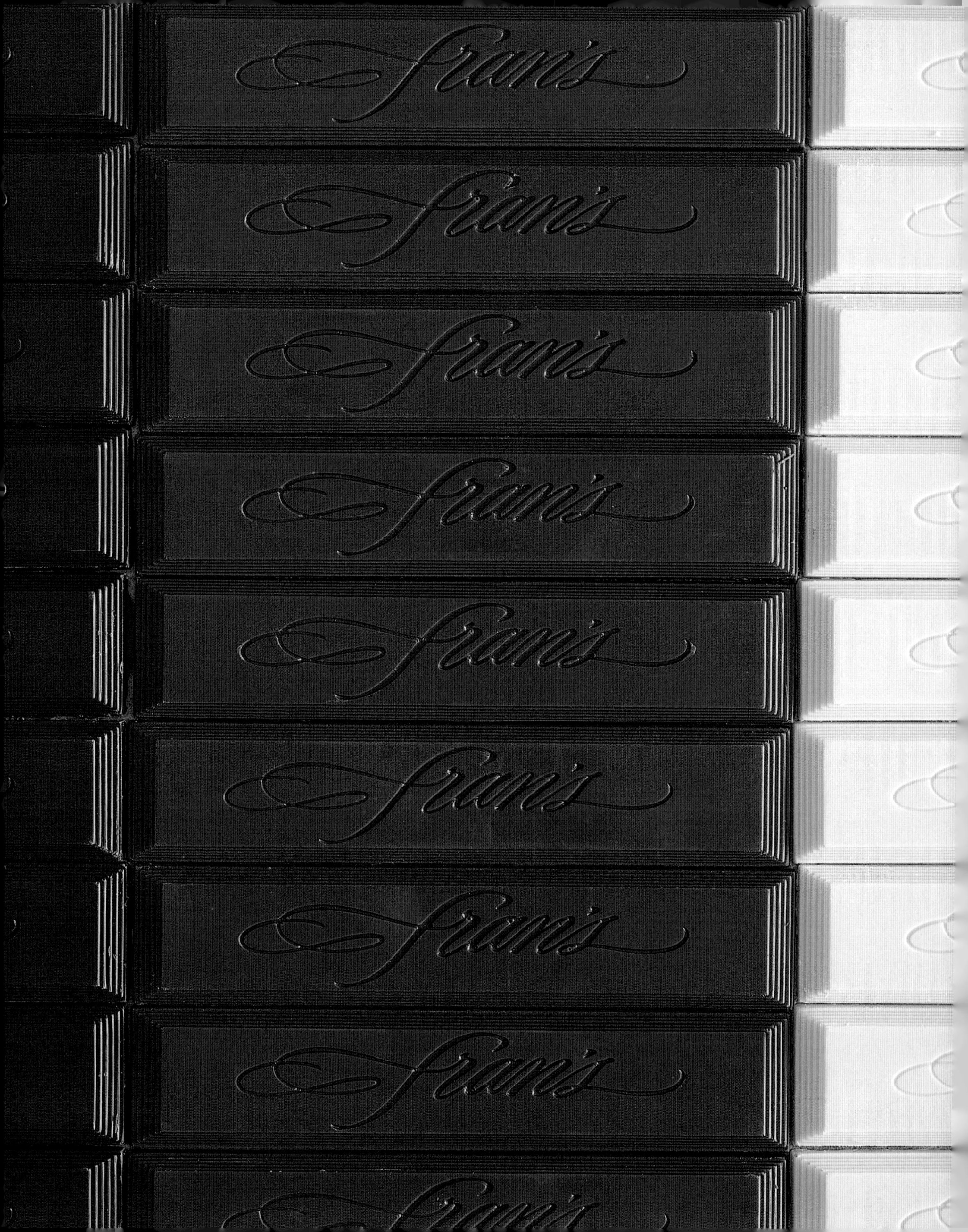
Fran's
Fran's
Fran's
Fran's
Fran's
Fran's
Fran's
Fran's

❧ prince torte layers ❧

A classic from the earliest days of the bake shop, this quintessential chocolate torte balances the denseness of dark chocolate with a light cake texture so that each bite dissolves and lingers on the palate. It is the building block for the four very special cakes that follow.

The Prince also makes an elegant single-layer torte—perfect for those who prefer a cake without nuts. Just divide the recipe in half and bake at 300°F in a 9-inch round pan for 35 to 40 minutes. You can dress it up with a shiny Chocolate Butter Glaze (page 214) or simply dust with cocoa. It is always sublime.

enough for two 9-inch round cake pans or two 9-by-13-inch (quarter-sheet) pans

12 ounces semisweet chocolate, finely chopped

¾ pound (3 sticks) unsalted butter, room temperature

8 large eggs, room temperature, separated

⅔ cups sugar

1 cup cake flour, sifted then measured

In a double boiler melt the chocolate over low heat. Remove the top of the boiler when the chocolate is nearly melted and continue stirring until completely smooth. Add the softened butter in 3 parts, stirring until no visible traces of butter remain. (If the butter begins to melt and separate, stop and allow the chocolate more time to cool.) The finished mixture should be glossy and smooth. Set aside to cool until the mixture is the consistency of softened butter. Briefly return to the double boiler if it begins to thicken too much.

In a mixer fitted with the whisk attachment, whip the egg yolks with half the sugar at medium-high speed, increasing to high speed until light and tripled in volume, 5 to 6 minutes.

Using a rubber spatula, fold the melted chocolate mixture into the egg mixture. The mixture should be smooth and glossy.

Meanwhile sift the flour again and set aside.

Clean the whisk, and in a clean bowl whip the egg whites on medium-high, increasing the speed to allow them to become quite frothy. Slowly add the remaining sugar and continue whipping until the peaks are stiff but not dry. The mixture should look glossy with a creamy consistency.

While the egg whites are finishing, fold the sifted flour into the chocolate mixture.

Lighten the chocolate mixture by quickly folding in a third of the whites, then gently fold in the remaining whites in 2 parts, trying not to overmix and lose the volume. Evenly spread the batter into the prepared pans and bake. Tightly wrap layers and refrigerate for up to 5 days, or freeze for one month prior to assembly.

⁘⟩ dylan's birthday cake ⟨⁘

If you want a cake to be loved, set aside the fruits, nuts, and liqueurs. Whether four or forty, most people want their chocolate cake straight, accompanied by a glass of milk or coffee. In my son Dylan's favorite cake, the crème fraîche hits just the right note to offset the extravagant richness. For a smaller cake, you can make one 9-inch layer and half the filling.

serves 24

1 recipe batter for Prince Torte Layers (page 94)

12 ounces bittersweet chocolate (preferably 66% cacao), finely chopped

24 ounces crème fraîche or sour cream

Position a rack in the middle of the oven and preheat the oven to 300°F. Lightly butter two 9-inch round cake pans (preferably flared) and line the bottoms with parchment paper circles.

Evenly spread batter for Prince Torte Layers into prepared round pans. Bake for 35 to 40 minutes, until the tops appear lighter in color and a tester inserted in the center comes out with moist crumbs. Allow the cake layer to cool in the pan at room temperature for approximately 10 minutes.

Turn the layers out of their pans (leaving the parchment attached) onto cardboard cake circles or tart bottoms and chill completely. (The cooled layers can be wrapped in plastic and frozen for up to a week prior to assembly.)

to make the filling/icing

In a double boiler melt the chocolate over low heat. Cool to lukewarm.

Put the crème fraîche in the bowl of an electric mixer fitted with a whisk attachment. On medium-high speed, whip the cream just to lighten, about 20 seconds. With the mixer on low speed, slowly add the melted chocolate, scraping the bowl often, until the mixture is creamy and glossy.

to finish the cake

Using a serrated knife, split the chilled layers horizontally. Place the bottom layer on the serving plate; remove the top cut layer and set aside. Spread approximately ½ cup of the crème fraîche icing on the first layer, about ¼ inch thick. Place the reserved layer on top, removing the parchment circle. Coat the layer with another ½ cup of icing. Repeat until all 4 layers are assembled with a cake layer on top. Trim any rough edges if necessary. Use the remaining icing to frost the top and sides of the cake. Refrigerate until set. Can be stored in the refrigerator for up to three days. Remove half an hour before serving.

Gilding the Lily: This cake is spectacular with the addition of the Dark-Chocolate Ganache Glaze (page 215). Prepare when the cake has chilled and follow the glazing instructions for La Rêverie (page 107).

❧ truffle torte ❧

The Truffle Torte is a celebration cake for the confirmed chocoholic. It is layer upon layer of semisweet chocolate cake and truffle filling, enrobed in a smooth, silky layer of semisweet chocolate ganache. The Truffle Torte has been described as a candy bar masquerading as a cake for good reason. It is a total chocolate experience.

serves 24

Dark-Chocolate Truffle Filling
(page 216)

1 recipe batter for Prince Torte
Layers (page 94)

Dark-Chocolate Ganache Glaze
(page 215)

Make the Dark-Chocolate Truffle Filling the day before baking and assembling the cake.

Position a rack in the middle of the oven and preheat the oven to 300°F. Lightly butter two 9-inch round cake pans (preferably flared) and line the bottoms with parchment paper circles.

Evenly spread the batter for Prince Torte Layers in the prepared round pans. Bake for 35 to 40 minutes, until the tops appear lighter in color and a tester inserted in the center comes out clean. Allow the cake layers to cool at room temperature in the pans for approximately 10 minutes.

Turn the layers out of their pans (leaving the parchment attached) onto cardboard cake circles or tart bottoms and chill completely. (The cooled layers can be wrapped in plastic and frozen up to a week prior to assembly.)

to finish the torte

Have ready the Dark-Chocolate Truffle Filling at room temperature, or the consistency of soft butter.

Remove the parchment from the torte layers. Using a long serrated blade, split the chilled layers in half horizontally. Remove the top of one layer and set aside.

With the bottom layer still on the cardboard cake circle or tart bottom, spread with approximately one quarter of the truffle filling, about ¼ inch thick. Top with the reserved layer and coat with truffle filling. Repeat until all 4 layers are assembled, with the top being a cake layer. Trim any rough edges if necessary. Use the remaining truffle filling to thinly coat and seal the top and sides of the cake. Chill the cake.

Let the Dark-Chocolate Ganache Glaze set about 30 minutes at room temperature, stirring occasionally until it thickens and ribbons off the end of the spatula, 80–85°F.

Place the cake (leaving it on the cardboard cake circle or tart bottom) on a cooling or pouring rack positioned over a rimmed baking sheet. (See pages 54–55.)

Beginning 1½ inches from the edge of the torte, slowly and evenly pour the glaze around the torte, making sure that the sides are sufficiently covered. Then pour the remaining glaze onto the center of the torte.

Working quickly, using a metal offset spatula, spread the glaze evenly over the top, letting the excess run down the sides.

Let set at room temperature until the glaze is slightly firm, about 20 minutes. Once set, slide an offset spatula under the card-board circle, rotating the spatula to release any spots where the glaze has stuck to the rack. Carefully lift the torte and, supporting the cake's bottom with your free hand, slide it onto its serving plate.

Can be stored in the refrigerator for up to 3 days. Remove half an hour before serving.

{ how to split a cake into layers }

Let your cakes cool before cutting into layers. To cut, place the cooled cake on a counter and visualize the height's midpoint. Then using a long serrated blade and a sawing motion, with one hand on top of the cake to turn it, make a 1-inch-deep cut all around the circumference of the cake. Once the cake is marked all the way around, gently push the blade through the center to cut in half horizontally, using the marks as your guide.

❊⁓{ marguerite torte }⁓❊

In the Marguerite a thin layer of tart dried apricots runs between the layers, cutting the richness of chocolate ever so slightly. This double-layer sheet cake is the easiest of the big cakes to assemble and serve, and it is a sure crowd pleaser. You can even cut it into 2-inch squares and set out on a tray for nibbling like petit fours. (For a smaller group you can halve the recipe and filling and bake it in a 9-inch round pan.)

It's named for my mother, Marguerite, who always cut such a stylish figure when she visited the original shop on weekends. Like the proper Seattle lady she is, she would show up for work early Saturday morning perfectly tailored, coifed, and made up. Then she would slip on an apron and hand out samples to those in line. After a morning spent wooing the public, Mom would slide into a seat at the counter and take a break over a cup of coffee and a slice of her favorite cake, the Marguerite.

Raspberry lovers—see the variation below. Both fruit fillings are jewel bright and would be lovely in bite-size tart shells.

serves 24

Dark-Chocolate Truffle Filling (page 216)

1 recipe batter for Prince Torte Layers (page 94)

1 double recipe Dark-Chocolate Ganache Glaze (page 215)

¼ cup (packed) roughly chopped dried California apricots (2 ounces)

¼ cup plus 2 tablespoons sugar

Make the Dark-Chocolate Truffle Filling the day before baking and assembling the cake.

Position a rack in the middle of the oven, and preheat the oven to 300°F.

Lightly butter two 9-by-13-inch or quarter-sheet pans and line bottoms with parchment paper.

Evenly spread the batter for Prince Torte Layers in the prepared sheet pans. Bake for 25 to 30 minutes, until the tops appear lighter in color and a tester inserted in the center comes out clean. Allow cake layers to cool at room temperature in the pan for approximately 20 minutes. (The layers can be wrapped in plastic once cooled and stored in the freezer up to a week prior to assembly. This size torte is easier to work with when well chilled.)

(continued)

to make the apricot filling

In a saucepan over medium-high heat, bring ½ cup water, the apricots, and the sugar to a simmer. Remove from the heat and cover, allowing the apricots to steep until plumped, about ½ hour. Put the apricot mixture into a food processor and purée until smooth. Set aside to cool.

to finish the cake

Have ready the Dark-Chocolate Truffle Filling at room temperature, or the consistency of soft butter.

Let the Dark-Chocolate Ganache Glaze set about 30 minutes at room temperature, stirring occasionally until it thickens and ribbons off the end of the spatula, 80–85°F.

Turn a cake layer out of its pan onto a 9-by-13-inch cardboard cake board. Peel away the parchment. Spread approximately three quarters of the chocolate truffle filling (about ¼ inch thick) over this layer, out to the edges. (If the truffle filling softens while spreading, return to the refrigerator for 5 minutes.)

Stir the apricot filling till smooth. Evenly spread a thin layer of the fruit filling over the truffle filling. Using a spatula, place the second chilled cake layer on top, parchment side up. Peel the parchment paper once it is positioned. Trim any rough edges if necessary. Use the remaining truffle filling to thinly coat the top and sides of the cake. Chill well.

Transfer the cake on its board to a cooling or pouring rack positioned over a rimmed baking sheet. (See pages 54–55.)

Beginning 1½ inches from the edge, slowly and evenly pour the glaze around the cake, making sure that the sides and corners are sufficiently covered. Then pour the remaining glaze onto the center of the torte. Working quickly, with a metal offset spatula spread the glaze evenly over the top, letting the excess run down the sides.

Let set at room temperature until the glaze is slightly firm, about 20 minutes. Once set, slide an offset spatula under the cardboard, rotating the spatula to release any spots where the glaze has stuck to the rack. Carefully lift the torte and, supporting the cake's bottom with your free hand, slide it onto its serving plate.

Can be stored in the refrigerator for up to 3 days. Remove half an hour before serving.

VARIATIONS

petit fours

raspberry filling

8 ounces fresh or thawed frozen raspberries

⅔ cup sugar

½ teaspoon lemon juice

In a saucepan over medium heat, bring all the ingredients to a simmer. Cook, stirring often to prevent scorching, until the mixture thickens, about 10 minutes. Strain through a fine-mesh sieve.

Set aside to cool.

To make petit fours like those pictured (page 99), chill the filled cake well. Using a warm, dry oval cutter (approximately 1-by-2 inches), carefully cut out the petit fours. Have the Dark-Chocolate Ganache Glaze ready. Dip the tops of the petit fours in the glaze and place on a sheet pan to set. May be decorated with a thin line of writing chocolate. Makes 24. Other shapes can easily be made by cutting with a warm, dry paring knife. Best eaten the same day as cut and glazed.

⁖{ blanc et noir }⁖

With its sharp corners and graphic black-and-white design, this modern layer cake is an elegant showstopper. For such a sophisticated-looking cake, the Blanc et Noir is surprisingly user friendly. It freezes well, cuts easily into thin clean slices, and is a melt-in-your-mouth delight. Each bite is like biting into a perfect baked truffle.

Even those who don't normally like white chocolate love the white chocolate ganache between its layers. It's much lighter than a buttercream and the taste is all chocolate, rather than the cloying sugary sensation you often get with fillings. It's worth shopping for a good-quality white chocolate like Valrhona. It makes all the difference.

serves 12 to 16

white-chocolate ganache filling

½ cup heavy cream

8 ounces white chocolate, finely chopped

noir cake layers

8 ounces semisweet chocolate, finely chopped

1 stick (8 tablespoons) unsalted butter, room temperature

5 large eggs, separated

½ cup plus 1 tablespoon sugar

1 recipe Dark-Chocolate Ganache Glaze (page 215)

white chocolate for writing

2 ounces white chocolate, roughly chopped

2 teaspoons vegetable oil

to make the filling

In a saucepan, heat the cream over medium-high heat just until it begins to boil. Remove from the heat and add the white chocolate, stirring until the chocolate is smooth and melted. Pour into a small bowl and cover with plastic wrap touching the surface to prevent a skin from forming. Let the ganache set up at least 12 hours or overnight at room temperature.

to make the cake

Position a rack in the middle of the oven and preheat the oven to 300°F.

Lightly butter a 9-by-13-inch or quarter-sheet pan and line with parchment paper. Then lightly butter the parchment paper.

(continued)

In a double boiler melt the chocolate over low heat. Remove the boiler top when the chocolate is nearly melted and continue stirring until completely smooth. Add the softened butter in 3 parts, stirring until no visible traces of butter remain. (If the butter begins to melt and separate, stop and allow the chocolate more time to cool.) The finished mixture should be glossy and smooth. Set aside to cool until the mixture is the consistency of softened butter. Briefly return to the double boiler if it begins to thicken too much.

In a mixer fitted with the whisk attachment, whip the egg yolks with half the sugar at medium-high speed, increasing to high speed until pale yellow and tripled in volume, 5 to 6 minutes.

Remove the bowl from the mixer. With a rubber spatula fold in the melted chocolate mixture. The mixture should be smooth and glossy.

Clean the whisk and in another clean bowl begin whipping the egg whites on medium-high speed, increasing the speed and allowing them to become quite frothy. Slowly add the remaining sugar and continue whipping until the peaks are stiff and creamy.

Lighten the chocolate mixture by quickly folding in a quarter of the whites until smooth and no traces of white remain. Then gently fold in the remaining whites in 3 parts, trying not to overmix and lose the volume. Evenly spread the batter into the prepared pan. The pan will be two-thirds full.

Bake for 20 to 25 minutes. The cake will rise above the edges of the pan, and a light crust will form on top. A cake tester inserted in the center will have a few moist crumbs.

Let the cake cool in the pan at room temperature for 10 minutes. Then chill until thoroughly cold, 4 hours or overnight. Wrap tightly with plastic wrap if chilling for longer than 4 hours. (The layer can be wrapped in plastic once cooled and placed in freezer up to a week prior to assembly.)

to assemble the cake

Have ready the White-Chocolate Ganache Filling.

To remove the well-chilled cake from the pan, run a thin-bladed knife around the edges. Place the bottom of a baking sheet over the cake and invert. Remove the parchment paper.

Place the filling in a mixing bowl. It should be the consistency of softened butter. (If not thick enough, stir and let sit longer to thicken.) With a whisk attachment or using a hand mixer, mix on high speed until the ganache is lighter in color and texture and soft peaks form, 2 to 4 minutes. Stop several times and scrape down the side of the bowl.

Using a ruler and the tip of a paring knife, mark the cake in thirds across its width. Cut the cake with a serrated blade into 3 approximately 4-inch-wide sections.

Place one chilled layer of the cake on the serving plate or on a 4-by-8-inch cardboard cake board. With a metal spatula, spread half of the white ganache filling on the layer. Top with the second chilled cake layer and spread with the remaining filling. Top with the last chilled cake layer.

Using a thin-bladed knife, trim the sides of the cake. Let set in the refrigerator at least 1 hour.

to finish the cake

Make the Dark-Chocolate Ganache Glaze.

Pour about ¼ cup of the glaze into a small bowl and place in the refrigerator to chill for approximately 25 minutes. Set aside the remaining ganache to cool about 30 minutes, gently stirring occasionally until it thickens and ribbons off the end of the spatula, 80—85°F.

Meanwhile make White Chocolate for Writing.

(continued)

to make writing chocolate

In a small bowl over simmering water, melt the chocolate. Remove from the heat, add the vegetable oil, and stir with a spatula until smooth. Set aside.

With an offset spatula, thinly coat the top and sides of the finished cake with the ¼ cup chilled ganache glaze. Transfer to a cooling or pouring rack positioned over a rimmed baking sheet.

Slowly and evenly pour the rest of the glaze around the sides of the cake, being careful to cover all the corners. Then pour the remaining glaze down the center using a metal spatula to spread the glaze evenly over the top, letting the excess run down the sides. Before glaze sets, decorate.

Pour the writing chocolate into a small parchment paper cone (page 24). Pipe 3 thin white parallel lines, ¼ inch apart, lengthwise, down the center of the cake over the soft glaze. Working quickly, with a toothpick draw small figure eights crosswise through the ganache and white stripes all along the cake's length.

Chill for 1 to 2 hours to set. Remove half an hour before serving. Can be stored in the refrigerator for up to 3 days.

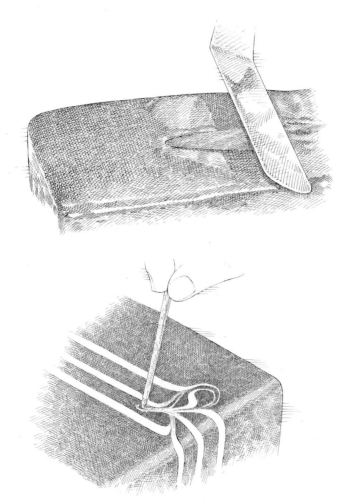

Glazing and decorating the Blanc et Noir

⁂⁅ mocha ricotta torte ⁆⁑

My version of the classic Italian Easter cake, Cassata Siciliana, features layers of chocolate torte interspersed with smooth, dense layers of chocolate-flecked ricotta. The key to a beautiful filling is to start with whole-milk ricotta. It whips up as thick as whipped cream and the flavor is much more interesting. Allow enough time in the refrigerator for all of the flavors to meld, and serve with a bowl of orange segments to pass around the table. A wonderful choice for a spring or summer gathering. For a smaller cake, you can simply make one 9-inch layer and half the filling.

serves 16

10 ounces semisweet chocolate, finely chopped

2 sticks plus 2 tablespoons unsalted butter, room temperature

1⅓ cups sugar

8 large eggs, separated

¼ cup double-strength coffee mixed with ¾ teaspoon instant espresso powder, room temperature

1⅓ cups (5⅓ ounces) almond flour (page 19)

1⅓ cups cake flour, sifted then measured

ricotta chocolate-chunk filling

1½ pounds whole-milk ricotta

3 tablespoons heavy cream

6 tablespoons sugar

3 tablespoons orange liqueur

2 ounces semisweet chocolate, finely chopped

2 ounces semisweet chocolate, grated, for decorating

Position a rack in the middle of the oven and preheat the oven to 300°F. Butter two 9-inch round cake pans and line with parchment paper circles.

In a double boiler melt the chocolate over low heat. Remove when nearly melted and continue stirring until smooth. Set aside and cool to 90°F. Return to the double boiler briefly if it begins to set up.

In a mixer fitted with the paddle attachment, at medium-high speed cream the butter with ⅔ cup of the sugar. The mixture will be pale yellow in color and fluffy with no grains of sugar remaining, 5 to 6 minutes. On medium speed, add the yolks one at a time, scraping the bowl with a rubber spatula between additions.

Remove the bowl from the mixer. With a rubber spatula fold in the double-strength coffee.

With a fork mix the almond and sifted flours together. Then, using a rubber spatula, fold into the yolk mixture. Fold in the melted chocolate. The mixture should be smooth and glossy.

(continued)

Clean the whisk and in another clean bowl begin whipping the egg whites on medium-high speed, increasing the speed until quite frothy. Slowly add the remaining sugar and continue whipping until the peaks are stiff but not dry. They will hold shiny peaks, and the mixture will have a glossy appearance and creamy consistency.

Lighten the chocolate mixture by quickly folding in one-third of the whites. Then gently fold in the remaining whites in 2 parts, trying not to overmix and lose the volume. Evenly spread the batter into the prepared pans.

Bake for 40 to 45 minutes, until the top appears lighter in color. A cake tester inserted in the center will have a few moist crumbs. Allow cake layers to cool at room temperature in the pan for approximately 15 minutes.

Turn each layer out of its pan onto a parchment-lined sheet pan or cake board and chill completely. (Once cooled, the layers can be wrapped in plastic and placed in freezer up to a week prior to assembly.)

to finish the torte

In a food processor fitted with a metal blade, blend the ricotta for 1 minute, until smooth. Or place a sieve over a mixing bowl and using the back of a rubber spatula, press the ricotta through.

Transfer the ricotta to a mixing bowl. Using a rubber spatula, fold in the cream and sugar until smooth. Fold in the orange liqueur and chopped chocolate.

Remove the cakes from the refrigerator or freezer. With a long serrated knife, evenly split the chilled layers in half horizontally.

Using a large spatula, gently lift off the top layer and transfer to the serving plate, removing the parchment paper. With an offset spatula, spread one-quarter of the ricotta filling on top of the layer, almost but not quite out to the edges. Repeat with remaining 3 layers, ending with a layer of filling on top.

Loosely cover with plastic wrap and place the torte in the refrigerator for 12 to 24 hours to allow the flavors to meld.

Before serving, dust the top with the grated chocolate.

With its fresh cheese filling, Mocha Ricotta Torte must be stored in the refrigerator. Remove up to a half hour prior to serving and do not keep out longer than 2 hours.

Gilding the Lily: For a more finished look, glaze with Dark-Chocolate Ganache Glaze (page 215). Fill between each cake layer with one-third of the ricotta chocolate chunk filling, omitting the top layer of filling. Let chill and mask and glaze with Dark-Chocolate Glaze, following instructions for La Rêverie (page 107).

❊{ la rêverie }❊

When my husband, Peter, who claims not to be a chocoholic, bit into this impressive layered walnut cake during testing for the book, he was immediately whisked back to the original Madison Street store and the cakes I used to make before chocolate took over my life. The inspiration was the Scandinavian Cloud Cakes that we grew up with in Seattle.

Peter likes his cakes light and clean, with chocolate more an accent than the dominant flavor. This one fits the bill. Four crunchy, airy layers of walnut cake interspersed with thin layers of white chocolate–spiked whipped cream and the thinnest, finest layer of smooth dark chocolate to hold it all together. It is Peter's new favorite birthday cake. serves 16 to 20

6 large eggs, room temperature, separated

1¼ cups sugar

1½ cups finely ground walnuts (about 5½ ounces)

1¼ cups finely ground dry ladyfingers (about 3½ ounces)

½ recipe White-Chocolate Whipped Cream (page 219)

¼ cup dark rum

Dark-Chocolate Ganache Glaze (page 215)

Position a rack in the middle of the oven and preheat the oven to 325°F.

Butter two 9-inch round cake pans (preferably flared) and line with parchment circles.

Using a mixer fitted with a whisk attachment, combine the egg yolks and half the sugar. Start whipping on medium-high speed. Once combined, scrape the sides of the bowl and increase the speed to high. Continue whipping until the mixture becomes thick, pale yellow in color, and the sugar has dissolved, about 5 to 6 minutes.

In a small bowl, with a fork stir together the finely ground walnuts and ladyfingers.

Using a rubber spatula, fold the walnuts and ladyfingers into the yolk mixture in 3 parts, making sure to thoroughly scrape the bottom of the bowl. The mixture will become very thick.

Clean the whisk and, in a clean mixing bowl, begin whipping the egg whites on medium-high speed, increasing the speed and beating until quite frothy. Slowly add the remaining sugar, continuously whipping until the peaks are stiff but not dry.

Lighten the yolk mixture by quickly folding in one quarter of the whites. Then gently fold in the remaining whites in

3 parts, trying not to overmix and lose the volume. Evenly spread the batter into the prepared pans.

Bake for 25 to 30 minutes, until light golden in color. A tester inserted in the center will come out dry. Allow cake layers to cool at room temperature in the pan for approximately 15 minutes.

Turn the layers out of their pans onto 9-inch cardboard cake circles or tart pan bottoms. Chill completely. (The layers can be wrapped in plastic once cooled and placed in freezer up to a week prior to assembly.)

to assemble the cake

Have ready the White Chocolate Whipped Cream filling in the refrigerator.

Unwrap the cake layers and remove the parchment. Using a serrated knife, split the torte layers in half horizontally. Remove the top layer of one cake and set aside.

With the bottom of one layer still on the cardboard cake circle or tart bottom, lightly brush the top with one quarter of the dark rum. Then spread approximately one-third of the White Chocolate Whipped Cream filling nearly to the edges. Top with the next layer, removing the parchment circle, and repeat layering with rum and cream filling until the last layer is brushed with rum. Trim any rough edges if necessary.

Loosely cover with plastic wrap and refrigerate for 3 to 6 hours.

to finish the cake

Make the Dark-Chocolate Ganache Glaze.

Pour about ¼ cup of the glaze into a small bowl and place in the refrigerator to chill for approximately 25 minutes. Allow the remaining ganache to cool about 30 minutes, gently stirring occasionally until it thickens and ribbons off the end of the spatula, 80 to 85°F.

With an offset spatula, thinly coat the top and sides of the finished cake with the chilled glaze. Transfer to a cooling or pouring rack positioned over a rimmed baking sheet. (See pages 54–55.)

Beginning 1½ inches from the edge of the cake, slowly and evenly pour the glaze around the cake, making sure that the sides are sufficiently covered. Then pour the remaining glaze onto the center. Working quickly, with a metal offset spatula spread the glaze evenly over the top, letting the excess run down the sides.

Chill in the refrigerator until the glaze is slightly firm, about 5 minutes. Once set, slide an offset spatula under the cardboard circle, rotating the spatula to release any spots where the glaze has stuck to the rack. Carefully lift the torte and, supporting the cake's bottom with your free hand, slide it onto its serving plate.

Store in the refrigerator. Remove up to half an hour prior to serving and do not keep out longer than 2 hours.

Gilding the Lily: La Reverie can be decorated by using excess ganache to pipe 16 rosettes with a #32 tip around the rim of the cake. Top each with a toasted walnut half. Writing chocolate (page 101) can also be used for a border; to make dark writing chocolate, simply substitute dark chocolate for the white.

❧ cappuccino cream cake ❧

The coffee-flavored whipped cream that crowns this elegant layer cake is reminiscent of the foam on a cappuccino. In fact, with its chocolate souffléed cake layers and simple whipped filling, the whole experience of taking a bite is as light and frothy as a good cappuccino. One of the easiest of the special occasion cakes to make, this one actually improves with a day in the refrigerator for the cake to absorb moisture from the filling.   serves 16 to 20

6 ounces bittersweet chocolate (preferably 70% cacao), finely chopped

6 large eggs, separated

½ cup plus 1 tablespoon sugar

3 tablespoons brewed cooled espresso or 3 tablespoons water mixed with 2 teaspoons instant coffee (preferably freeze-dried)

Cappuccino Whipped Cream (page 220)

dark Dutch-processed cocoa powder for dusting

Position a rack in the middle of the oven and preheat the oven to 325°F.

Lightly butter a 9-by-13-inch or quarter-sheet pan and line with parchment paper. Lightly butter the parchment paper.

In a double boiler melt the chocolate over low heat. Remove when nearly melted and continue stirring until smooth. Set aside.

In a mixer fitted with the whisk attachment or using a hand mixer, combine the egg yolks and half the sugar and start whipping on medium-high speed. Once combined, scrape the sides of the bowl and increase the speed to high. Continue whipping until the mixture becomes thick, pale yellow in color, and the sugar has dissolved, 5 to 6 minutes.

Clean the whisk and in another clean bowl, begin whipping the egg whites on medium-high speed, increasing the speed until quite frothy. Slowly add the remaining sugar and continue whipping until the peaks are stiff but not dry.

Pour the cooled coffee into the melted chocolate all at once and quickly stir together to prevent seizing. If it does thicken and start to separate, don't worry. Constant stirring will make it smooth and creamy.

Lighten the chocolate mixture by folding in one-third of the yolks. Then add the lightened chocolate mixture to the remaining yolks and gently fold. The mixture will become light and airy with large air bubbles where some traces of yolk remain. That is okay.

Lighten the yolk mixture by quickly folding in one-quarter of the whites, then gently fold in the remaining whites in 3 parts, trying not to overmix and lose the volume.

Pour the glossy dark chocolate batter into the prepared pan, smoothing the top. The pan will be more than three-quarters full. Bake for 20 to 25 minutes, until the top is domed in the center and dry to the touch. A tester inserted in the center will come out dry and clean with a few crumbs. Let cool in the pan at room temperature. The layer will pull away from the sides of the pan as it cools.

to finish the cake

Have ready the Cappuccino Whipped Cream filling in the refrigerator.

To remove the cooled cake, run a thin-bladed knife around the edges of the pan. Place the bottom of a baking sheet lined with parchment over the cake and invert. Peel the parchment paper.

Using a ruler and the tip of a paring knife to mark the cake, divide into 3 equal sec-tions across the width. Cut the cake with a serrated blade to make 3 layers about 4 inches wide.

Place one chilled cake layer on a serving plate. With a metal spatula, spread one third of the filling over the layer, gener-ously overlapping the edges. Repeat with second layer and a layer of filling. (The layers of filling should be equal in height to a cake layer.) Top with the last chilled cake layer. Being careful not to overwork the cream, frost the top and sides with the remaining cappuccino cream, swirling the top. Refrigerate at least 4 to 6 hours to set the cake and meld the flavors. Before serving, dust with cocoa powder. Can be stored in the refrigerator for up to 2 days.

VARIATION

For a children's layer cake, omit the coffee and fill the layers with sweetened whipped cream (page 218).

{ how to cut a cake }

*t*he best knife for cutting clean slices without creating a cake wreck is a long serrated blade. I always keep a tall glass or pitcher of hot tap water nearby, along with a towel. Just warm the blade by dipping in the water. Then wipe it off with the towel and cut a slice. I recom-mend dipping and drying the blade be-tween each slice to keep the blade warm.

As for the dilemma of cutting equal portions of a round cake, here's a strat-egy. Make the first cut down the middle to divide the cake in half. Then cut one quarter and decide how many slices you want to get from the cake, dividing that quarter into thirds or quarters depend-ing on your needs. Follow suit with the remaining quarters.

l'étoile

After my professional pastry training, I grew tired of French-style genoises that are traditionally soaked in syrup or liqueur for added flavor. I wanted a more delicious white cake that would derive intense flavor and moisture from white chocolate.

This lovely all-white version is a favorite at our retail stores in the summertime and also forms the basis for many of our wedding cakes. It was the cake my daughter, Andrina, chose for her wedding.   serves 12

12 ounces white chocolate, finely chopped

1 stick plus 2 tablespoons unsalted butter, room temperature

¾ cup sugar

6 large eggs, room temperature, separated

½ cup cake flour, sifted then measured

3 tablespoons almond flour (page 19)

1½ cups crème fraîche

Position a rack in the middle of the oven and preheat the oven to 300°F.

Lightly butter a 9-inch round cake pan and line the bottom with a parchment paper circle.

In a double boiler melt 6 ounces of the white chocolate over low heat. Cool to lukewarm.

In a mixer fitted with the paddle attachment, cream the butter with half of the sugar on medium-high speed until light, scraping the bowl often, about 2 minutes.

Add the egg yolks, one at a time, waiting until each yolk is incorporated before adding the next. Continue beating until the sugar is dissolved, about 3 minutes total. Pour in the melted chocolate and mix until smooth and glossy. Set aside.

Blend the sifted flour with the almond flour. Gently fold into the chocolate mixture.

In another clean bowl of the mixer, with a clean whisk begin whipping the egg whites on medium-high speed, increasing the speed and allowing them to become quite frothy. Slowly add the remaining sugar and continue whipping until the peaks are stiff but not dry.

Lighten the white-chocolate-and-nut mixture by quickly folding in one-quarter of the whites, then gently fold in the remaining whites in 3 parts, trying not to overmix and lose the volume. Evenly spread the batter into the prepared pan.

Bake for 50 minutes, until lightly golden in color and a tester inserted in the center comes out clean. Cool in the pan, at room temperature, for about 10 minutes.

(continued)

Turn the layer out onto a 9-inch cardboard cake circle or metal tart bottom and cool completely. (Once cooled, the cake can be wrapped in plastic and placed in the freezer for up to a week prior to assembly.)

to finish the cake

In a double boiler melt the remaining white chocolate over low heat. Cool to lukewarm.

Place the crème fraîche in the bowl of an electric mixer fitted with the whisk attachment. Whip the cream on medium-high speed, just to lighten it, about 20 seconds. It will appear to mound in the bowl. Remove from the mixer and with a rubber spatula fold in the melted white chocolate. The mixture should be creamy with a velvety texture.

Using a serrated knife, split the torte horizontally into 2 layers.

Remove the top cut layer. Spread about a third of the icing on the bottom layer. Top

with the second cake layer. Center, trim the rough edges if necessary, and remove the parchment circle.

Use the remaining icing to cover and frost the top and sides of the cake. Refrigerate until set, about 4 hours. Store in the refrigerator. Remove at least half an hour before serving. Can be stored for up to 3 days.

VARIATIONS

For a Scandinavian Cloud Cake, spread the layers with lingonberry jam alternating with white chocolate whipped cream. Or add a layer of sliced strawberries between the layers.

To make a two-tier celebration cake as pictured on page 113, double the recipe. Divide the batter evenly between two 9-inch round cake pans and two 6-inch round cake pans. Assemble as per instructions. Chill well. Place the 9-inch cake on a serving platter. Center and place the 6-inch layer on top. Decorate with rose petals or candied flowers if desired.

{ decorating with candied flowers }

i love the natural look of candied flowers on a cake. Even if they may never be eaten, all of the items used for candying should be edible. Look for organic, pesticide-free roses, pansies, and violets from the garden. All are lovely to look at against a glossy chocolate glaze. It takes about a day for sugared items to dry, so you want to plan ahead for special occasions.

For flowers, pinch off the stems and carefully pull apart the petals. Using

pasteurized egg whites or dry, reconstituted whites, whisk with a fork until slightly frothy. Hold each piece in your fingertips and with a small paintbrush dab with the beaten whites until each surface is covered. Dip in a bowl of granulated sugar to evenly coat all over and place on a cooling rack, with air circulating above and below, to dry overnight.

Candied flowers can be stored in airtight containers for several months.

❧ triple chocolate pyramid ❧

For those organized enough to plan their cakes in advance, the pyramid cake offers multiple rewards. First there's the taste—perfectly balanced layers of dense, moist chocolate sponge perfumed with almonds, alternating with a rich, creamy milk-chocolate filling. Then there are the spectacular visuals. The pyramid is fabulous with a row of sparklers down the middle for New Year's Eve or a sophisticate's birthday party. And last but not least important for the baker is the fact that the Triple Chocolate freezes, stores, and ships so well. In a square shape, I've sold it in our catalog for years. It is virtually indestructible.

If you do have any Triple Chocolate left over, you want to wrap it well and stash in the freezer. I've been told that an ice-cold slice, eaten straight out of the freezer, is one of life's great (and chewy) midnight snacks. serves 18 to 24

1½ sticks (12 tablespoons) unsalted butter, room temperature

¾ cup sugar

8 ounces almond paste, cut into small pieces, room temperature

4 large eggs, room temperature

⅔ cup Dutch-processed cocoa powder, measured then sifted

Milk-Chocolate Hazelnut Filling (page 217)

1½ recipes Dark Chocolate Ganache Glaze (page 215)

Position a rack in the middle of the oven and preheat the oven to 300°F.

Lightly butter two 9-by-13-inch or quarter-sheet pans and line with parchment paper. Lightly butter the top of the parchment paper.

In a mixer fitted with the paddle attachment, beat the butter and sugar on medium-high speed until light and fluffy, 4 to 5 minutes. Scrape down the sides of the bowl several times.

Reduce the speed to medium and slowly add the almond paste, a piece at a time. Continue beating, increasing speed to high, until smooth, 4 to 5 minutes. Stop and scrape down the sides of the bowl several times.

At medium speed, add the eggs, one at a time, thoroughly mixing between each addition. The mixture will be light, fluffy, and pale yellow in color.

Remove the bowl from the mixer, and with a rubber spatula gently fold in the cocoa.

Divide the batter and pour into the prepared pans, smoothing the top. The pans will be one-quarter full. These are thin layers.

(continued)

Bake for 20 to 22 minutes, or until the cake loses its shine and springs back when lightly touched. The finished cake will start pulling away from the sides of the pan. As the cake cools, it will continue to shrink.

Place the torte layers in the refrigerator to chill.

to assemble the cake

Make the Milk-Chocolate Hazelnut Filling. While it whips remove the torte layers from the refrigerator. Run a thin knife around the edges of the cakes to loosen.

To remove, cover the cake with a sheet of parchment. Top with another clean baking sheet and invert so the cake in the pan releases onto the sheet pan. Repeat with the second cake layer. Remove the parchment paper from each layer.

Using a ruler and the tip of a knife to make a mark, measure across the width to divide each layer in half. With a sharp blade cut each layer in half lengthwise, making 4 dense layers, about 4 by 12 inches each.

Cut a cake board to 4 by 12 inches and with a spatula transfer a layer to the board.

Evenly spread about a quarter of the Milk-

Chocolate Hazelnut Filling over the layer, so that the filling and the cake are each about ¼ inch thick. Repeat until all the layers are assembled and the top layer is filling. The finished height should be approximately 2 inches.

With a metal spatula, smooth the sides. Chill for 1 to 2 hours to set. (At this point the cake can be glazed as a loaf, similar to the Blanc et Noir, page 101. For a more elaborate presentation, forge ahead and make the pyramid.)

to form the pyramid

The concept for making a pyramid is to slice a rectangular loaf along the diagonal into 2 parts and then press together the 2 long triangles to make a larger triangle. You'll need a long thin slicing knife or serrated blade, dipped in hot water and wiped dry, to gracefully complete this maneuver.

Place the chilled cake on its board along the edge of the counter lengthwise. Align your blade at the upper left rear corner of the loaf and the lower right bottom corner, resting the blade on the counter. With a firm slicing motion (not sawing back and forth) cut the cake in half along the diagonal into 2 even triangular strips. Use the

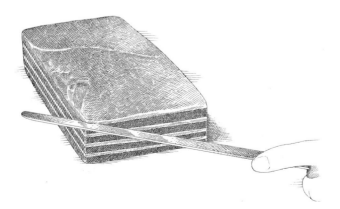

Cutting the pyramid cake on the diagonal.

Assembled pyramid cake.

{ cake storage and serving }

My favorite place to keep a cake is on a counter, where folks can marvel at its beauty and pinch a slice. Most of the cakes can stay at room temperature up to three days without appreciable loss of flavor. However, if you do bake far in advance, you will need to refrigerate or freeze. Think about where you place it in the fridge, since chocolate is a great absorber of other flavors. Always let a frosted cake firm up for a few hours, uncovered, in the refrigerator. Then loosely wrap with plastic, being careful not to disturb the smooth finish.

For the very best flavor I like to return baked items to room temperature before serving. Whipped cream cakes are the exception. If a torte or cake has been frozen, partially thaw in the refrigerator about 6 hours before placing on a counter to return to room temperature. Gradually defrosting reduces condensation and results in a better-looking cake.

Once a cake has been cut, you can keep it moist by tightly covering the exposed edges with plastic wrap. Before serving, trim and discard the thinnest slices on the ends if they look dry.

cardboard and counter as a guide for your knife, and be careful not to position your fingers in front of the blade.

Stand one triangle on its short side, removing any parchment. Stand the second triangle and position back-to-back to form a larger triangle, with the filling layer touching the cake layer in the middle. Transfer to a 3-by-12-inch cake board and press firmly together. The finished torte should be about 3 inches wide, 4 inches tall, and 12 inches long. Transfer to the refrigerator and chill until firm.

to finish the cake

Make the Dark-Chocolate Ganache Glaze.

Pour about ½ cup of the glaze into a small bowl, and place in the refrigerator to chill for approximately 25 minutes. Set aside the remaining glaze to cool about 30 min-

utes, gently stirring occasionally until it thickens and ribbons off the end of the spatula, about 80–85°F.

With an offset spatula, thinly coat the sides and ends of the finished torte with the chilled glaze. Transfer to a cooling or pouring rack positioned over a rimmed baking sheet.

Slowly and evenly pour the glaze over the ends of the torte, being careful to cover all the corners. Then pour the remaining glaze on both sides, using a metal spatula to spread if necessary. Let set about 15 minutes. Transfer to a serving plate.

Fill a pastry bag fitted with a #18 tip with the thickened glaze from the baking sheet. Pipe a small shell border down the top of the torte.

Store in the refrigerator. Remove at least half and hour before serving. Can be stored for up to 3 days.

ROLLED CAKES AND BÛCHES DE NOËL

Once you try making one of these rolled cakes, you'll be hooked. Rolls are a wonderful choice for serving a large party because they look so elegant on a platter and they keep their good looks as they sit. Guests can help themselves by simply cutting across the roll. It's impossible to wreck such a neat little package.

All of these rolls can be dressed up or down according to the occasion. For Christmas they each can become the ultimate rolled cake, the bûche de Noël. See page 121 for technique tips for making a traditional Yule log.

Rolled cakes—essentially a light cake layer wrapped around a cream filling—follow a similar formula. For best results, bake the cake and fill it a day in advance. Before rolling, always let the cake cool to room temperature in the pan. Then, after rolling, chill overnight to set. Pour the chocolate glaze the next day, just before serving.

Rolled cakes are flexible concepts. Whipped cream, mousses, and buttercreams all make excellent fillings for a roll, and your favorite nut can be substituted for the choices in the cake layers that follow. The trick is to jump in and start rolling.

cakes on the move

It takes some strategy to transport your painstakingly prepared, perfect cake creations. Sunshine can be a chocolate cake's worst enemy—take it from someone who has witnessed a wedding-cake meltdown. In the car, turn on the air conditioner and place delicate cakes and chocolates out of direct sunlight. Use a few loops of masking or Scotch tape to hold the bottom of the cakeboard to the serving platter or box and position it on the floor where you can keep an eye on it. As you drive, try to take turns slowly and avoid steep hills and quick stops. The true strategist should print a map before setting out. Chocolate has no patience for getting lost.

milk-chocolate hazelnut roll

Here is one to satisfy all the milk-chocolate lovers. My most popular holiday bûche combines a crunchy, nutty sponge layer with a rich gianduja filling.

serves 16 to 20

6 large eggs, room temperature, separated

¾ cup sugar

¾ cup finely ground hazelnuts (3 ounces)

¾ teaspoon baking powder

Milk-Chocolate Hazelnut Filling (page 217), room temperature

Position a rack in the middle of the oven and preheat the oven to 325°F.

Lightly butter a 9-by-13-inch or quarter-sheet pan and line with parchment paper. Lightly butter the parchment paper.

Using a mixer fitted with the whisk attachment, combine the egg yolks and half of the sugar. Start whipping on medium-high speed. Once combined, scrape the sides of the bowl and increase the speed to high, whipping until the mixture becomes thick, pale yellow in color, and the sugar has dissolved, 5 to 6 minutes.

In a small bowl, toss together the hazelnuts and baking powder.

Using a rubber spatula, fold the nuts into the yolk mixture in 3 parts. The mixture will become thick.

Clean the whisk, and in a clean mixing bowl begin whipping the egg whites on medium-high speed, increasing the speed and allowing them to become quite frothy. Slowly add the remaining sugar and continue whipping until the peaks are stiff but not dry.

Lighten the yolk mixture by quickly folding in one-quarter of the whites. Gently fold in the remaining whites in 3 parts, trying not to overmix and lose the volume. Spread the batter into the prepared pan.

Bake for 25 to 30 minutes, until golden brown and the top is puffy and feels dry to the touch. A tester inserted in the center will come out dry. Let cool at room temperature in the pan for about 30 minutes. The cake falls and pulls away from the sides as it cools. Leave in the pan for assembly.

to finish the roll

Run a sharp paring knife along the edges of the pan to loosen. Using the knife, trim excess on all 4 edges to make the cake level. Leave the sponge layer in the pan.

Spread half the Milk-Chocolate Hazelnut Filling evenly over the cake layer, leaving 1 inch of cake bare along the outside edges. Using the parchment to lift, start rolling the cake lengthwise, tucking the cake and peeling back the parchment as you go. Transfer the roll to a serving platter.

With the remaining filling frost the exposed sides and ends of the roll, swirling with an offset spatula. The finished roll should be approximately 3 inches in diameter and 12 inches in length. Chill to set. Store in the refrigerator. Remove at least half an hour before serving. Can be stored for up to 3 days.

turning a rolled cake into a bûche de noël

*a*ny of the rolled filled cakes can be turned into a festive Yule log or bûche de Noël for the holidays. My favorite at Christmas is the traditional Chestnut Cream Roll. Here are a few techniques—any and all are optional. First, prepare any of the rolled cakes up to and including glazing and chill well. Reserve the excess glaze.

To make meringue mushrooms: the day before assembling prepare the batter for Chocolate Meringues on page 37, omitting the 4 ounces bittersweet chocolate. Using a 1/2-inch round tip, pipe about ten 1 3/4-inch round disks, about 3/4 inches tall, for the mushroom caps. Then pipe the same number of stems, about 1 1/4 inches round at the base tapering to a pointed tip, about 2 inches tall. Dust the tops of the mushroom caps with powdered sugar, or cocoa, and bake following the directions in the recipe.

To assemble the mushrooms when cool, melt about 6 ounces semisweet chocolate to no more than 90°F. Using the point of a sharp paring knife, scrape out a small cone hole about 1/4 inch deep in the middle of the cap's bottom. Dip the bottom in the melted chocolate to evenly coat, wiping off excess with a finger. Then dip the pointy tip of each stem piece

about 1/4 inch deep in the chocolate. Press the tip of each stem into the hole in each cap's center and set aside to set.

To form branches, you will need the excess glaze that has gathered in the sheet pan after glazing. The glazed cake should be well chilled before decorating. Using a warm, dry slicing knife, trim a 2-inch-long chunk along the diagonal from both ends of the log and set aside for branches. Transfer the log to a serving platter.

Press one branch, glaze-to-glaze, along the side on one end of the log. Using the leftover glaze as "cement," with a spatula patch the cracks between log and branch. Place the second branch on the other end of the log, pointing up, glaze-to-glaze, and use the excess glaze to patch. I prefer to leave the exposed branch ends uncovered, but they can also be covered with glaze at this point. (Cover the exposed ends with plastic wrap until serving.)

Using a decorating comb and delicate sweeping motions in the same direction, draw tree-trunk lines through the glaze on the log.

Decorate the combed log with meringue mushrooms, a sprinkling of milk-chocolate curls (page 14), and a dusting of powdered sugar.

❧ chestnut cream roll ❧

Crème de marrons, a sweetened purée of glacéed chestnuts, enriches each part of this traditional French bûche. Serve European-style in thin slices since the taste is so exquisitely rich and intense. Though I've never been a big chestnut fan, I came to understand the French obsession with this starchy nut after experimenting with the crème version in desserts. This recipe uses the whole 17-ounce can of crème de marrons.   serves 16 to 20

5 large eggs, separated

¼ cup sugar

9 ounces (¾ cup plus 2 tablespoons) canned sweetened chestnut cream (crème de marrons)

½ cup fine dry bread crumbs

chestnut cream filling

¾ cup heavy cream, chilled

8 ounces (⅔ cup) canned sweetened chestnut cream (crème de marrons) or the remainder from the 17-ounce can

Dark-Chocolate Ganache Glaze (page 215)

Position a rack in the middle of the oven and preheat the oven to 325°F.

Lightly butter a 9-by-13-inch or quarter-sheet pan and line with parchment paper. Lightly butter the parchment paper.

With the whisk attachment of a standing mixer or using a hand mixer, combine the egg yolks and half of the sugar and whip starting on medium-high speed. Once combined, scrape the sides of the bowl and increase the speed to high. Continue whipping until the mixture becomes thick, pale yellow in color, and the sugar has dissolved, 5 to 6 minutes. Remove from the mixer.

Fold the chestnut cream into the yolk mixture.

Clean the whisk, and in another clean bowl begin whipping the egg whites on medium-high speed, increasing the speed and allowing them to become quite frothy. Slowly add the remaining sugar and continue whipping until the peaks are stiff but not dry. They should appear glossy and smooth.

Lighten the yolk mixture by quickly folding in a quarter of the whites. Then, alternating with the bread crumbs, gently fold in the remaining whites in 3 parts, trying not to overmix and lose the volume. Spread batter evenly into the prepared pan. It will be three-quarters full.

Bake for 20 to 25 minutes, until slightly domed and lightly golden in color. A tester inserted in the center will come out clean. Allow the cake layer to cool in the pan at room temperature.

to assemble the roll

Make the chestnut cream filling. Either by hand or using a mixer, lightly whip the cream until it just mounds in the bowl.

Add the chestnut cream to the lightly whipped cream. Whisk by hand until thoroughly combined and peaks form, taking care not to overwhip the cream. You want a soft, creamy texture.

Leaving the cooled sponge layer in the pan, spread the chestnut cream filling evenly over the cake, leaving 1 inch bare along both longer sides. Begin to roll the layer toward the uncovered edge, loosening the parchment from the sponge only enough to continue rolling. The finished roll will be approximately 3 inches in diameter and 12 inches in length. Wrap the roll in the loosened parchment and chill 3 to 6 hours before glazing.

to finish the cake

Have ready the Dark-Chocolate Ganache Glaze.

Pour about ¼ cup into a small bowl and place in the refrigerator to chill for approximately 20 minutes. Allow the remaining ganache to cool at least 30 minutes, stirring occasionally until it thickens and ribbons off the end of the spatula, 80–85°F.

Using a spatula, place the roll on a cardboard cake board cut to roughly 2¾-by-12-inches. (Slightly smaller than the roll.) Thinly coat the top, sides, and ends with the chilled glaze. Transfer the board to a cooling or pouring rack positioned over a rimmed baking sheet.

Beginning at the end of the roll, slowly and evenly pour the reserved glaze down the length of the roll, making sure that the sides and ends are sufficiently covered.

If necessary, use a metal offset spatula to spread the glaze evenly over the top, letting the excess run down the sides. Let set 5 minutes and transfer to serving platter. Refrigerate for longer storage.

{ chocolat au chocolat roll }

This double chocolate roll is as easy to make as it is to eat. Its five simple ingredients should be staples in most baker's kitchens. The Chocolate Sour-Cream Ganache is a real find for the pastry maker in a hurry. In a minute or two you have an excellent, easy-to-handle filling for tart shells and layer cakes.

serves 16 to 20

4 ounces bittersweet chocolate (preferably 70% cacao), finely chopped

4 large eggs, separated

¼ cup plus 2 tablespoons sugar

2 tablespoons brewed espresso or 2 tablespoons water mixed with 1 teaspoon instant coffee or espresso

chocolate sour-cream ganache

6 ounces bittersweet chocolate, finely chopped

1 cup sour cream

Dark-Chocolate Ganache Glaze (page 215)

Position a rack in the middle of the oven and preheat the oven to 325°F.

Lightly butter a 9-by-13-inch or quarter-sheet pan and line with parchment paper. Lightly butter the parchment paper.

In a double boiler melt the chocolate over low heat. Remove the top of the boiler when chocolate is nearly melted and continue stirring until smooth.

With the whisk attachment of a standing mixer or using a hand mixer, combine the egg yolks and half of the sugar by whipping on medium-high speed. Once combined, scrape the sides of the bowl and increase the speed to high. Continue whipping until the mixture becomes thick, pale yellow in color, and the sugar has dissolved, 5 to 6 minutes.

In another clean bowl with a clean whisk or beaters, begin whipping the egg whites on medium-high speed, increasing the speed and allowing them to become quite frothy. Slowly add the remaining sugar and continue whipping until the peaks are stiff but not dry.

Pour the coffee into the melted chocolate all at once and quickly stir together to prevent chocolate from seizing. If it begins to separate, don't worry. Constant stirring will bring it back to a smooth, creamy mass.

Lighten the chocolate mixture by folding in one-third of the yolks. Then add the lightened chocolate mixture to the remaining yolks and gently fold together. The mixture will become light and airy with large air bubbles where some traces of yolk remain.

Lighten the yolk mixture by quickly folding in a quarter of the whites. Then gently fold in the remaining whites in 3 parts, trying not to overmix and lose the volume.

Pour the glossy dark-chocolate batter into the prepared pan, smoothing the top. The pan will be three-quarters full. Bake for 20 to 25 minutes, until the top is domed in the center and dry to the touch. A tester inserted in the center will come out dry and clean with a few crumbs. Let cool at room temperature in the pan. As it cools, the layer will pull away from the sides of the pan.

to assemble the roll

Make the Chocolate Sour-Cream Ganache.

In a double boiler melt the chocolate over low heat. Remove from the heat and stir until smooth. Cool to lukewarm.

Place the sour cream in the bowl of an electric mixer. With a whisk attachment on medium-high speed, whip the cream just to lighten, about 20 seconds. It will appear to mound in the bowl. With the mixer on low speed pour in the melted chocolate, scraping the bowl often. The mixture should be velvety in texture.

Leaving the sponge layer in the pan, spread the Chocolate Sour-Cream Ganache filling evenly over the cake layer, leaving 1 inch of the cake bare along the length of the longer sides. Begin to roll the layer toward the uncovered edge, loosening the parchment from the sponge only enough to continue rolling. The finished roll will be approximately 3 inches in

diameter and 12 inches in length. Wrap the roll in the loosened parchment and chill 3 to 6 hours before glazing.

to finish the cake

Have ready the Dark-Chocolate Ganache Glaze.

Pour about ¼ cup into a small bowl, and place in the refrigerator to chill for approximately 20 minutes. Allow the remaining ganache to cool at least 30 minutes, stirring occasionally until it thickens and ribbons off the end of the spatula, 80–85°F.

Place the roll on a cardboard cake board cut to roughly 2¾ by 12 inches (slightly smaller than the roll). Thinly coat the top, sides, and ends with the chilled glaze. Transfer the board to a cooling or pouring rack positioned over a rimmed baking sheet.

Beginning at the end of the roll, slowly and evenly pour the glaze down the length of the roll, making sure that the sides and ends are sufficiently covered.

If necessary, use a metal offset spatula to spread the glaze evenly over the top, letting the excess run down the sides. Let set 5 minutes and transfer to serving platter. Serve at room temperature. Refrigerate for longer storage, up to 3 days.

⁕⟩ tropicale coconut roll ⟨⁕

I made an important discovery back at the original store. I found that when I infused white-chocolate ganache with coconut, it suddenly became a grownup version of the filling of my favorite childhood candy bar—the Mounds bar. I've covered this luxuriously smooth confection with dark chocolate to make the Coconut Gold Bar and used it as the center in my favorite Easter egg. In the Tropicale, it provides the perfect creamy contrast to a thin nutty cake layer and an elegant dark-chocolate glaze. The Tropicale is perfect for an Easter buffet.

serves 16 to 20

¾ cup heavy cream

¾ cup unsweetened dried shredded coconut

8 ounces white chocolate, finely chopped

4 ounces unsalted macadamia nuts

½ cup plus 1 tablespoon sugar

4 large eggs, separated

1 teaspoon baking powder

to make the filling

In a saucepan, heat the cream over medium-high heat just until it begins to simmer. Remove from the heat, add the coconut, and let steep for 3 minutes to infuse. Add the white chocolate and stir until the chocolate is smooth and melted. Pour the ganache into a small bowl and cover with plastic wrap touching the top. Let set at room temperature at least 5 hours or as long as 24 hours.

to make the cake

Position a rack in the middle of the oven and preheat the oven to 325°F.

Lightly butter a 9-by-13-inch or quarter-sheet pan and line with parchment paper. Lightly butter the parchment paper.

Place the macadamia nuts with 1 tablespoon of the sugar in a food processor fitted with the steel blade. Pulse until finely ground, remove, and set aside.

With the whisk attachment of a standing mixer or using a hand mixer, whip the egg yolks with ¼ cup sugar on medium-high speed. Once combined, scrape the sides of the bowl and turn the speed to high, whipping until the mixture becomes thick, pale yellow, and the sugar has dissolved, 5 to 6 minutes.

In a small bowl, toss together the macadamia nuts and the baking powder. Add to the yolk mixture and gently fold.

In another clean bowl, with a clean whisk or beaters, start whipping the egg whites on medium-high speed. Increase the speed to high and whip until quite frothy, slowly adding the remaining sugar. Continue whipping until the peaks are stiff but not dry.

(continued)

Lighten the yolk mixture by quickly folding in a quarter of the beaten whites. Gently fold in the remaining whites in 3 parts, trying not to overmix and lose volume. Pour batter into the prepared pan and spread evenly.

Bake for 20 to 25 minutes, until lightly golden in color and a tester inserted in the center comes out with moist crumbs. Allow cake to cool in the pan at room temperature. Cover with plastic wrap and chill as long as 5 hours.

to assemble the roll

While the layer is still well chilled, place the coconut ganache in a mixing bowl. With a paddle attachment of a standing mixer or a hand mixer, beat at medium speed, scraping the sides of the bowl often. Beat until the ganache is lighter in both color and texture, less than 1 minute.

Unwrap cake. Leaving the sponge layer in the pan, spread the coconut ganache filling evenly over the cake layer, leaving 1 inch of the cake bare along one of the longer sides. Begin to roll the layer toward the uncovered edge, loosening the parchment from the sponge only enough to continue the rolling process. The finished roll will be approximately 3 inches in diameter and 12 inches in length. Wrap the roll in the loosened parchment and chill 3 to 6 hours before glazing.

to finish the cake

Have ready the Dark-Chocolate Ganache Glaze.

Pour about ¼ cup into a small bowl and place in the refrigerator to chill for approximately 20 minutes. Allow the remaining ganache to cool at least 30 minutes, stirring occasionally until it thickens and ribbons off the end of the spatula.

Place the roll on a cardboard cake board cut to roughly 2¾ by 12 inches (slightly smaller than the roll). Thinly coat the top, sides, and ends with the chilled glaze. Transfer the board to a cooling or pouring rack positioned over a rimmed baking sheet.

Beginning at the end of the roll, slowly and evenly pour the glaze down the length of the roll, making sure that the sides and ends are sufficiently covered.

If necessary, use a metal offset spatula to spread the glaze evenly over the top, letting the excess run down the sides. Let set 5 minutes and transfer to serving platter. Refrigerate for longer storage.

Gilding the Lily: The remaining glaze can be placed in a pastry bag fitted with a star tip. A decorative border can be applied to the top of the roll.

{ sumptuous cheesecakes, puddings, and custards }

belgian-chocolate cheesecake

When I started developing a cheesecake for the original store, I wanted the distinctive flavor of dark chocolate to dominate. That meant increasing the proportion of chocolate to cheese in the typical cheesecake recipe and then experimenting to find the perfect dark chocolate, one that would behave when combined with the other ingredients while retaining its rich flavor. I found the answer—a full-bodied, 56 percent Belgian chocolate that remains one of my all-time favorites for baking. If you can't find it, substitute another chocolate in the 56 to 60 percent range. The cacao percentage is really more important than origin.

There are two moments to be most vigilant when blending ingredients for a cheesecake, because your batter must be absolutely lump-free. The first is when you beat together the cheese with the sugar. The second is when adding the melted chocolate. You want to make sure that no bits of warm chocolate splash onto the sides of the bowl, where they will harden into those dreaded lumps—the kind that do not dissolve in baking.

serves 16

1 pound semisweet chocolate (preferably 56% cacao by Callebaut), finely chopped

1½ pounds cream cheese, room temperature

⅔ cup sugar

4 large eggs, room temperature

whipped heavy cream or Chocolate Crème Anglaise (page 173) for serving

Position a rack in the middle of the oven and preheat the oven to 300°F.

Butter and line a 9-inch round cake pan with parchment paper.

In a double boiler melt the chocolate over low heat. Remove the top of the boiler when the chocolate is nearly melted and continue stirring with a rubber spatula until smooth. Cool the chocolate to 90°F, stirring occasionally.

In a mixer with the paddle attachment, beat the cream cheese at medium-high speed until smooth, about 2 minutes. Add the sugar and continue beating for an additional 3 minutes, scraping down the sides of the bowl several times, until the sugar is dissolved and the mixture is light, fluffy, and smooth. It should be entirely free of lumps with the consistency of sour cream.

(continued)

In a small bowl, gently whisk together the eggs. With the mixer on low speed, slowly add half of the eggs, stopping and scraping down the sides of the bowl. Continue mixing, adding the remaining eggs.

Still on low speed, slowly pour the melted chocolate into the center of the bowl, being careful not to let the chocolate splash on the sides of the bowl. Remove the bowl from the mixer, and scrape down the sides with a rubber spatula. Fold the mixture by hand until no traces of white remain. The mixture will thicken as you fold in the chocolate.

Pour into the prepared pan, smoothing the top. The pan will be approximately three-quarters full. Place the pan on a heavy-duty rimmed baking sheet, and transfer to the oven. Pour approximately ½ inch of simmering water into the baking sheet for a bain-marie. Bake for 55 to 65 minutes, or until the edges pull away from the sides of the pan and the top appears dull.

Let cool in the pan for 2 to 4 hours.

To remove the cake, run a thin blade around the edges to loosen. Place a piece of parchment or waxed paper over the top and invert the cake onto a plate. Peel the parchment paper round from the bottom and turn the cake onto its serving plate. Remove the top parchment. Serve at room temperature with Chocolate Crème Anglaise (page 173) or unsweetened whipped cream. This may be stored in the refrigerator as long as 1 week.

❧ brie white-chocolate cheesecake ☙

When one of my staff bakers couldn't stop raving about a Brie cheesecake she had tasted on a vacation trip, I became obsessed. After working on the recipe for weeks and bringing in far too many cheesecakes, I finally hit it— this white-chocolate version of a French cheesecake. (She later told me that it far surpassed the cake that she remembered.) It went on to become a favorite at Fran's.

It has a more complex flavor than most cheesecakes because it uses two cheeses and the texture is pure lightness. The trick is to whip each cheese separately, until they are of equal texture, and then blend. serves 16

4 ounces white chocolate, roughly chopped

1½ pounds cream cheese, room temperature

12 ounces ripe Brie cheese, room temperature (preferably 40% butterfat), weighed after the rind is removed

¾ cup sugar

5 large eggs, room temperature

Position a rack in the middle of the oven and preheat the oven to 300°F.

Lightly butter a 9-inch round cake pan. Line bottom with a lightly buttered parchment paper circle.

In a double boiler melt the white chocolate over low heat. Remove the top of the boiler when the chocolate is nearly melted and stir until completely smooth. Set aside to cool.

In a mixer with the paddle attachment, beat the cream cheese at medium-high speed until smooth, about 3 minutes. Transfer the cheese from the mixing bowl to another bowl and set aside.

In the same mixing bowl using the paddle attachment, on medium-high speed beat the Brie until completely smooth and elastic, about 3 minutes, scraping the bowl often with a rubber spatula.

With the machine on medium speed, add the cream cheese to the Brie in 3 parts. Blend the cheeses together until smooth, scraping down the sides of the bowl. Reduce speed to low and slowly add the sugar.

At medium speed, add the eggs, one at a time, scraping down the sides of the bowl as necessary.

On low speed, pour the melted white chocolate into the middle of the bowl. Mix until well blended, smooth, and creamy.

Pour into the prepared pan. Place pan on a heavy-duty rimmed baking sheet and place on the rack in the oven. Pour about ½ inch of simmering water into the baking sheet to form a bain-marie.

Bake, uncovered, for 1 hour and 15 minutes, or until the top is lightly golden brown and puffed. The center should no longer jiggle when the pan is moved.

Let cool in pan for 2 to 4 hours.

To remove the cake, run a thin blade around the edges to loosen. Place a piece of parchment or waxed paper over the top of the cake and invert it onto a plate. Peel the parchment paper round from the bottom and turn the cake onto its serving plate. Remove the top parchment paper. Serve with seasonal berries or Raspberry Sauce (page 175). May be stored in the refrigerator for as long as 1 week.

❧{ cheesecake secrets }❧

*a*ll of your cheesecakes should start with totally softened cream cheese. You can even let the cheese sit overnight. If you must start with cheese right out of the refrigerator, break into pieces and, about 10 to 15 minutes before beginning the recipe, beat with the paddle until soft and smooth.

Sometimes, no matter how diligently you beat, a few hardened bits of cheese will cling to the sides of the bowl. Avoid the temptation to scrape them down into the batter at the last moment. Better to lift them out with your fingers and toss them away, since those stubborn little bits are never going to dissolve in baking.

If your cheesecakes get messy when serving, just remember to drag your warm, dry knife along the bottom of the board when cutting rather than pulling the knife (and all that cheese) back up through the cake.

chocolate hazelnut cheesecake

I created this cheesecake for milk-chocolate lovers. It has just the right balance of tang from the cream cheese and added flavor from the nuts to avoid one-note sweetness. If you prefer your chocolate taste pure, simply skip the nuts and use 14 ounces of milk chocolate—the darkest you can find. Glazing with silky dark chocolate, though not absolutely necessary, adds yet another chocolate dimension. In spite of how it may sound, this creamy cheesecake is not overly rich.

serves 16

14 ounces gianduja (page 20), finely chopped, or 9 ounces 36–46% cacao milk chocolate, finely chopped, and 5 ounces hazelnut paste

4 ounces semisweet chocolate, finely chopped

1½ pounds cream cheese, room temperature

½ cup sugar

5 large eggs, room temperature

3 tablespoons heavy cream

3 tablespoons Frangelico or Amaretto liqueur

Dark-Chocolate Ganache Glaze (page 215) (optional)

Position a rack in the middle of the oven and preheat the oven to 300°F. Butter a 9-inch round cake pan and line with parchment paper.

In a double boiler over low heat, melt the gianduja (or milk chocolate with hazelnut paste) and semisweet chocolate. Remove the top of the boiler when the chocolate is nearly melted and continue stirring until smooth. Let the chocolate cool to 90°F, stirring occasionally.

In a mixer fitted with the paddle attachment, beat the cream cheese at medium-high speed until smooth, about 2 minutes. Add the sugar and continue beating for an additional 3 minutes, until the sugar is dissolved and the mixture is light, fluffy, and lump-free. Stop several times to scrape down the sides of the bowl.

In a small bowl whisk together the eggs. Turn the mixer speed to low and slowly add half of the eggs. Stop, scrape down the sides of the bowl, and continue mixing, adding the remaining eggs. Pour in the cream and Frangelico, and thoroughly mix on low.

Remove the bowl from the mixer and with a rubber spatula fold in the melted chocolate. Continue folding until no traces of the cream cheese remain. The mixture will thicken as you fold in the chocolate.

Pour into the prepared pan, smoothing the top. The pan will be about three-quarters full. Place on a rimmed baking sheet and place in the oven. Pour about ½ inch of simmering water into the baking sheet for a bain-marie. Bake for 1 hour and 10 minutes, until the top is smooth and slightly dull. The edges should start to pull away from the sides of the pan.

Let cool at room temperature for 2 to 4 hours.

To remove the cake, run a thin knife around the edges to loosen. Place a piece of parchment or waxed paper over the top of the cake and invert it onto a plate. Remove the parchment paper round from the bottom and turn the cake right side up onto its serving plate. Remove the paper from the top.

If you are adding the glaze, set the room-temperature cake on a cake board. Place on a rack over a baking sheet. Have the glaze ready.

When the glaze reaches 80–85°F, beginning 1½ inches from the edge of the cake, slowly and evenly pour the glaze around the rim, making sure that the sides are sufficiently covered. (See pages 54–55.) Then pour the remaining glaze onto the center of the cake. Working quickly, using a metal offset spatula, spread the glaze evenly over the top, letting the excess run down the sides.

Let set at room temperature until the glaze is slightly firm, about 20 minutes. Once set, slide an offset spatula under the board, rotating the spatula to release any spots where the glaze has stuck to the rack. Carefully lift the cake and, supporting the bottom with your free hand, slide it onto its serving plate. May be stored in the refrigerator as long as 1 week.

❧ chocolate crème brûlée ❧

Experimenting with classic vanilla custard with a burnt sugar crust gave me an excuse to focus on two of my favorite flavors, chocolate and caramel. I used a higher percentage of bittersweet chocolate to offset the sugary topping, making this as addictive a custard as you will ever encounter. Heat just brings out the nuances and intensifies the chocolate's seductive qualities.

The classic shallow ovals for making crème brûlée are the best because they create just the right proportion of custard to crust. If you don't have a butane torch, crème brûlée can be caramelized under the broiler. Just dust with extra sugar and position about 4 inches from the flame. Turn the custards frequently to avoid burnt spots.

serves 6

5 egg yolks

¼ cup sugar, plus an additional 6 tablespoons sugar for caramelizing

2 cups heavy cream

½ vanilla bean, split lengthwise

4½ ounces bittersweet chocolate (preferably 70% cacao), finely chopped

Position a rack in the middle of the oven and preheat the oven to 300°F. Have ready six 7-ounce shallow, oval ramekins or crème brûlée dishes.

In a small bowl, combine the egg yolks with 2 tablespoons of the sugar. Gently whisk, without beating in air, until smooth and the sugar begins to dissolve. Set aside.

In a large heavy saucepan heat the cream with the split vanilla bean and 2 tablespoons sugar until it comes to a simmer. Remove from the heat. Lift out the vanilla bean and let cool a minute. Holding the bean over the cream, gently scrape loose all the seeds with the back of a paring knife so they fall into the pot. Discard the empty pod or rinse and let dry for vanilla sugar. (Place the dried pod in a sugar canister.) Stir in the chocolate until thoroughly melted and smooth.

Pour one-third of the chocolate mixture into the egg mixture and stir to combine. Then add the remaining chocolate mixture, gently stirring until smooth.

Strain the custard through a fine-mesh sieve into a large measuring cup. Pour about 3 ounces into each ramekin, about ½ inch deep. Firmly tap the base of each cup on the counter to remove any bubbles.

Arrange the ramekins in a heavy-rimmed baking sheet or roasting pan. Put the baking dish into the oven and fill with ½ inch simmering water for a bain-marie.

(continued)

sumptuous cheesecakes, puddings, and custards

Bake the custards for 20 minutes, or until set. The tops should be glossy and the surface should move evenly when shaken. If the center moves independently, return to the oven. With a wide spatula, lift and transfer the custards to a rack to cool. Then transfer to the refrigerator to thoroughly chill, 2 to 4 hours, uncovered.

About an hour before serving, sprinkle a tablespoon of sugar over each chilled custard. Holding a propane or butane torch several inches from the surface, begin passing the flame back and forth until the sugar begins to melt and caramelize. Your goal is a thin crisp crust so that each bite of custard is accompanied by a bite of caramel.

Refrigerate to set the crust, about 30 minutes but not too long. Lengthy refrigeration will cause the caramel to weep. For the creamiest consistency, serve at room temperature.

VARIATION

Small, deep ramekins or custard cups can also be used for crème brûlée. You need to adjust the time since they will take longer to bake—as long as 15 minutes more for 3-ounce ramekins. Cover the pan with aluminum foil to prevent a crust from forming during longer baking time. Thin porcelain is always best for baking.

sumptuous cheesecakes, puddings, and custards

❧ princess pudding ❧

When I was invited to teach a class with nothing more than a hot plate as equipment, I came up with this unbelievably rich, pure chocolate pudding, a miracle of simplicity. It can be made on the stovetop in under 15 minutes. My friend Julie named it because it is a pudding fit for a princess, or some very lucky guests.

It's gorgeous served in elegant demitasse cups or mounded in martini glasses and topped with a dollop of whipped cream. The pudding can also be poured into baked miniature tart shells.   serves 8

1¼ cups heavy cream

½ cup sugar

½ vanilla bean, split lengthwise

5 large egg yolks

7 ounces semisweet chocolate, finely chopped

Cappuccino Whipped Cream (page 220) for serving

In a small saucepan, combine the cream and sugar. Using the back of a paring knife, scrape the vanilla bean seeds into the mixture. Toss in the bean. Place over medium heat and bring just to a simmer. Remove from the heat.

In a mixing bowl, whisk the egg yolks until frothy. Slowly pour one-third of the cream into the yolks, whisking constantly. Pour the mixture back into the pan and return to low heat. Cook, stirring constantly, until the mixture coats the back of a spoon (about 160°F).

Remove from the heat. Remove and discard the vanilla bean. Add the finely chopped chocolate and whisk until melted and smooth.

While mixture is still warm, pour into a serving bowl or into 8 individual demitasse cups. Let cool slightly, then top with loosely whipped cappuccino cream and serve.

Princess Pudding is best served at room temperature, to bring out the chocolate flavor. It can be refrigerated as long as 2 days.

❧ chocolate pots de crème ❧

Having grown up on my grandmother's homemade chocolate puddings, I feel strongly that home-cooked pudding deserves a revival. Nothing compares to a silky smooth, rich custard for soothing the day's existential wounds. I've taken Grandma's version into the twenty-first century by using a fine bittersweet chocolate and creating a consistency thick enough to stand a spoon in.

If you're new to pudding making, a custard such as this one, gently baked in the oven rather than stirred on the stovetop, is virtually foolproof. It's a great, easy addition to anyone's dessert repertoire.

serves 6

1 whole egg

5 egg yolks

2 tablespoons plus 1 teaspoon sugar

pinch of salt

1 cup heavy cream

1 cup whole milk

8 ounces semisweet chocolate (preferably 60% cacao), finely chopped

Position a rack in the middle of the oven and preheat the oven to 300°F. Have ready six 5-ounce pot de crème cups or ramekins about 3½ inches in diameter.

In a medium bowl combine the egg and yolks with 1 tablespoon plus 1 teaspoon of the sugar and the pinch of salt. Whisk until smooth and the sugar begins to dissolve. Set aside.

In a large heavy saucepan heat the cream, milk, and remaining sugar until it comes to a simmer. Remove from the heat and add the finely chopped chocolate. Gently stir until the chocolate is melted and smooth.

Pour about one-third of the chocolate mixture into the eggs and stir to combine. Then add the remaining chocolate mixture, gently stirring without beating in air until smooth.

Strain the custard through a fine-mesh sieve into a large measuring cup. You should have about 24 fluid ounces. Pour about 4 ounces into each pot de crème cup or ramekin until ½ inch from the top. Firmly tap the base of the cups on the counter to remove any bubbles.

Place the lids on the pot de crème cups or individually cover the ramekins tightly with plastic wrap to prevent a skin. With a skewer or tip of a knife, punch a small hole in the surface of the plastic wrap for a vent. Arrange the custards in a heavy-rimmed baking dish or roasting pan. Place in the oven and pour boiling water to a depth of 1 inch for a bain-marie. If using ramekins, cover the pan loosely with foil.

Bake for 35 minutes, or until the custard is set. The tops should be glossy and the surface should move evenly when shaken. If the center moves independently, continue baking.

Pots de crème are irresistible served warm out of the oven, but they can also be made ahead and refrigerated. Let warm to room temperature before serving.

{ chilled spectaculars }

❧ chocolat au chocolat ice cream ❧

My inspiration for the ice creams I sell at the shops are the dense spoonfuls of perfection that I remember first tasting at Berthillon in Paris. Since chocolate ice creams often aren't distinct enough for my tastes, I use deep, dark cocoa to enrich and underline that pure chocolate note. It's very important to totally cook out the raw taste of cocoa so it doesn't leave a dry taste on the tongue. An assortment of flavorful ice creams, served in small oval scoops formed by two soup spoons, is always a perfect ending to an elegant dinner.

makes 1 quart or 8 generous servings

⅔ cup Dutch-processed cocoa powder, sifted

½ cup sugar

1½ cups whole milk

1½ cups heavy cream

6 large egg yolks

5 ounces semisweet chocolate, finely chopped

1½ teaspoons pure vanilla extract

3 tablespoons Kahlua

In a heavy saucepan whisk together the cocoa powder and half of the sugar. Slowly pour in ½ cup of the milk and whisk until a smooth paste is formed. Whisk in the remaining milk and cream.

Place the saucepan over medium-low heat. Cook, stirring frequently, about 10 minutes, or until the raw taste of cocoa has disappeared. Do not let the cocoa mixture come to a simmer or boil. Remove from the heat.

In a large mixing bowl whisk together the remaining sugar and egg yolks. Slowly pour about 1½ cups of the warm cocoa mixture into the yolks, stirring constantly. Then pour the yolk mixture back into the saucepan, stirring constantly, to prevent the eggs from forming curds.

Return to low heat. Cook, stirring constantly, until the mixture begins to thicken and coats the back of a spoon (about 160°F). Remove from the heat and add the chocolate. Let sit 1 minute to melt the chocolate. Then stir until smooth. Stir in the vanilla and Kahlua.

Cover with plastic touching the top so a skin does not form. Let cool to room temperature and refrigerate until cold.

Freeze in an ice-cream maker following the manufacturer's directions.

ICE-CREAM SERVINGS

My ice creams are extremely dense and freeze to a solid consistency. The best way to serve them is to warm on a counter about 10 minutes to soften. The ideal texture offers some resistance to a scoop but is not rock hard.

⁂⧽ almost burnt sugar ice cream ⦃⁂

For the most intense caramel flavor, practice cooking the sugar just far enough, so that it turns a deep, dark brown—a blink short of burning. The trick is to stay nearby and keep testing by spooning a few drops on a white plate. You want to pull it off the heat the moment before the sugar goes from dark brown to black. Unfortunately, there is no turning back with burnt caramel.

This very rich ice cream has the golden color of a caramel apple and a totally smooth consistency. Its taste is pure caramel with a subtle scent of vanilla. It's superb with Pure Chocolate Sauce (page 170) or Caramel Sauce (page 177).

makes 1 quart or 8 generous servings

½ vanilla bean, split lengthwise

2 cups whole milk

2 cups heavy cream

½ cup plus 2 teaspoons sugar

8 large egg yolks

In a heavy saucepan combine the vanilla bean, milk, and cream and whisk together. Cook over medium-low heat, stirring frequently, until it comes to a simmer. Remove from the heat. Lift out the vanilla bean and, with a paring knife, gently scrape any remaining seeds back into the cream mixture. Discard the bean or save for vanilla sugar. Return the pan with the cream mixture to a burner over medium-low heat.

Place the sugar in a small nonstick pan. Cook over low heat until it begins to melt and continue cooking, stirring frequently with a wooden spoon or heat-resistant spatula, until the sugar is completely melted and clear. Increase the heat to medium-high and cook until it reaches a deep brown. (If you have trouble seeing the color change against the dark surface of the pan, spoon a few drops onto a white dish to test.) Slowly pour the caramelized sugar into the warm cream, stirring until completely smooth. If the caramel begins to solidify, turn up the heat and cook until it dissolves. Remove from the heat.

In a mixing bowl whisk the egg yolks. Slowly pour in about 1½ cups of the warm caramelized cream mixture, stirring constantly. Then pour the yolk mixture back into the saucepan, stirring continuously.

Return the pan to medium heat. Cook, stirring constantly, until the mixture begins to thicken and coats the back of a spoon, about 160°F. Remove from the heat and pour through a fine-mesh sieve into a bowl.

Cover the custard with plastic touching the top to prevent a skin from forming. Refrigerate until cold.

Freeze in an ice-cream maker following the manufacturer's directions.

{ ginger key lime ice cream }

In my quest for interesting flavors to serve with Pure Chocolate Sauce (page 170), I played with several contrasting combinations. This is an all-time favorite. Hot spicy ginger, tart lime, and sweet white chocolate hit all the right notes to bring out the best in bittersweet chocolate. Look for moist, chewy candied ginger—Baker's Cut crystallized Ginger Chips by Ginger People is a good choice—for the best results.

makes about 1 quart or 8 generous servings

6 ounces candied ginger

1½ cups whole milk

2 cups plus 3 tablespoons heavy cream

¼ cup sugar

6 large egg yolks

9 ounces white chocolate, finely chopped

2 tablespoons key lime juice, fresh or bottled (page 20)

Finely chop half of the crystallized ginger into ¼-inch pieces. Place the remaining ginger in a small food processor or blender. Purée until smooth. Set aside.

In a heavy saucepan whisk together the milk, 1½ cups of the cream, and the finely chopped ginger. Cook over medium-low heat, stirring frequently, until mixture comes to a simmer. Remove from the heat and let steep for 10 minutes. Pour through a fine-mesh sieve into a bowl, discarding the ginger.

Pour the liquid back into the pan and return to the heat. Bring barely to a simmer and remove from the heat.

In another bowl, whisk together the sugar and egg yolks. Slowly pour about 1½ cups of the warm-milk mixture into the yolk mixture, stirring constantly. Then pour the yolk mixture back into the saucepan, stirring continously.

Return the pan to medium heat. Cook, stirring constantly, until the mixture begins to thicken and coats the back of a spoon, about 160°F.

Remove from the heat and add the white chocolate. Let sit 1 minute to melt the chocolate. Then stir until completely smooth. Stir in the key lime juice, the remaining cold cream, and the puréed candied ginger.

Cover the custard with plastic touching the top to prevent a skin from forming. Refrigerate until cold.

Freeze in an ice-cream maker following the manufacturer's directions.

⋅⦚ white-chocolate coconut ice cream ⦚⋅

As crazy as I am about coconut, I found I could get great flavor and texture by just relying on canned coconut milk. For an ice-cold version of the Coconut Gold Bar, add a thin coating of Deepest, Darkest Chocolate Sauce (page 172) and a sprinkling of toasted, shaved coconut on top. To toast thick unsweetened coconut strips, heat in a 325°F oven until the edges are golden, about 5 minutes.

makes about 1 quart or 8 generous servings

1½ cups whole milk

1½ cups heavy cream

¼ cup plus 1 teaspoon sugar

6 large egg yolks

9 ounces white chocolate, finely chopped

a 5½-ounce can unsweetened coconut milk

In a heavy saucepan whisk together the milk, cream, and 1 teaspoon of the sugar. Cook, stirring frequently, over medium-low heat until the mixture comes to a simmer. Remove from the heat.

In a large mixing bowl whisk together the remaining sugar and egg yolks. Slowly pour about 1½ cups of the warm milk mixture into the yolk mixture, stirring constantly. Then pour the yolk mixture back into the saucepan, stirring constantly.

Place the pan over medium-low heat. Cook, stirring constantly, until the mixture begins to thicken and coats the back of a spoon, about 160°F.

Remove from the heat and add the white chocolate. Let sit 1 minute to melt the chocolate. Then stir until completely smooth. Stir in the coconut milk.

Cover the custard with plastic touching the top to prevent a skin from forming. Refrigerate until cold.

Freeze in an ice-cream maker following the manufacturer's directions.

VARIATION

For a pure, silky white-chocolate ice cream, simply replace the coconut milk with the same amount of heavy cream stirred in at the end.

❈{ ultimate ice-cream sandwiches }❈

During the summer, I like to nab some Chocolate Wafers from the shop so I can stock my home freezer with homemade ice-cream sandwiches for our outdoor barbecues. Maybe that's the reason my grown children keep dropping by after dinner! One Seattle fan is so hooked that she ordered 250 ice-cream sandwiches for her summer wedding reception.

makes 6 large ice-cream sandwiches

½ recipe Chocolate Wafers
(12 baked cookies) (page 39)

1 pint favorite ice cream, softened
or freshly churned

Bake and cool the cookies according to the recipe.

Place a small scoop of soft ice cream on the bottom of one of the cookies. Cover with a second cookie bottom side down and gently press to make a sandwich.

Repeat until all 6 sandwiches are made and place in the freezer immediately. Freeze until completely hard, at least 2 hours.

To store, individually wrap in plastic or put in an airtight container in the freezer.

❈⟨ milk-chocolate sorbet ⟩❈

My goal in making a milk-chocolate sorbet was to pack in a maximum of flavor without losing the milk chocolate's smooth, creamy texture. Using the blender ensures a silky consistency, with all the particles of fat completely emulsified. I think you'll like the way freezing accentuates the chocolate flavor while taming the sweetness of milk chocolate.

makes about 1 quart or 8 generous servings

½ cup sugar

3 cups water

1 pound plus 6 ounces milk chocolate, finely chopped

2 ounces unsweetened chocolate, finely chopped

½ teaspoon pure vanilla extract

In a heavy saucepan combine the sugar and water. Cook over medium-high heat until it begins to simmer.

Remove from the heat and add the chocolates. Let sit 1 minute to melt the chocolates. Then stir until completely smooth. Stir in the vanilla.

Set aside to cool further until warm to the touch. Then pour into a blender and cover tightly. Blend on high speed until smooth, about 1 minute. Pour into a bowl and cover with plastic wrap touching the top.

Set aside to cool further about 30 minutes, until the mixture is just at room temperature. If it sits too long, it will become too thick to churn, so keep a watchful eye.

Freeze in an ice-cream maker following the manufacturer's directions.

ᔬ} pure chocolate sorbet {ᔮ

Just in case today's fudgesicles aren't as grand as you remember from child-hood, this luxurious version ought to bring you right back to those carefree days. This dark, rich sorbet tastes like a frozen hot chocolate.

makes about 1 quart or 8 generous servings

½ cup plus 1 tablespoon sugar

¼ cup plus 2 tablespoons Dutch-processed cocoa powder, sifted

3½ cups water

1 pound plus 6 ounces bittersweet chocolate, finely chopped

½ teaspoon pure vanilla extract

Sift together the sugar and the cocoa powder and transfer to a heavy saucepan. Slowly pour in ½ cup of the water, whisking constantly until a smooth paste is formed. Whisk in the remaining water.

Place the saucepan over medium-low heat. Cook, stirring frequently, until the mixture comes to a boil. Remove from the heat and add the chopped chocolate. Let sit 1 minute to melt the chocolate. Then stir until completely smooth. Stir in the vanilla. Cover with plastic wrap touching the top.

Set aside to cool about 30 minutes, until the mixture is just at room temperature. If the mixture sits too long it will become too thick to churn, so keep a watchful eye.

Freeze in an ice-cream maker following the manufacturer's directions.

⁂⧽ ice-box cake ⧼⁂

I remember being thrilled whenever my mother whipped up this classic 1950s fantasy of whipped cream and chocolate wafers. The sight of it always meant we were in for a celebration. I haven't added anything to detract from the perfect yin-yang of snowy white cream and dark-chocolate cookies. Pay attention when whipping the cream so it remains loose enough to spread and be absorbed.

serves 16 or more

18 Chocolate Wafers (page 39)

2 cups heavy cream, chilled

¼ cup sugar

1 teaspoon pure vanilla extract

frosting

1 cup heavy cream, chilled

2 tablespoons sugar

½ teaspoon pure vanilla extract

dark-chocolate curls for decorating (page 14)

Have ready the Chocolate Wafers, cooled.

Line an 8½-by-4½-inch loaf pan with a single piece of parchment paper covering bottom and sides.

Whisk the cream until it becomes quite thick. Add the sugar and vanilla. Continue whisking until soft peaks form. Be careful not to overwhip the cream, since it must remain loose enough to be absorbed by the cookies.

to assemble the cake

Evenly spread about ¾ cup of the whipped cream over the bottom of the parchment-lined pan.

Spread a spoonful of whipped cream about ¼ inch thick on 2 wafers. Stand them upright, cream-side-out, across the width of the pan, to form 2 rows. Repeat with each cookie, coating and pressing to sandwich ¼ inch of cream between the cookies in 2 rows. The last wafer should be coated on both sides with whipped cream. Spread the remaining whipped cream over the top and ends of the loaf to completely cover the cookies. Straighten the top by running a metal spatula over it.

Cover with plastic wrap and chill for 12 to 24 hours.

to finish the cake

Make the frosting. Whisk the cream until it becomes quite thick. Add the sugar and vanilla, and continue whisking until soft peaks form, being careful not to overwhip.

Unwrap the cake. Place a cake board or serving tray on top and invert to remove the cake. Remove the parchment. Scoop the freshly whipped cream onto the top of the cake. Using an offset spatula, frost the top and sides, swirling into peaks on the top. Chill for 2 to 4 hours before serving.

Shower with dark-chocolate curls to decorate.

dark-chocolate mousse

Now that restaurant desserts have become multilayered extravaganzas, it's rare to find a simple bowl of fabulously rich, silken chocolate mousse on a menu. It's a shame, because mousse is so deeply satisfying when all you crave is a small spot of chocolate at the end of a meal. As the French know, it really is the perfect last-minute homemade dessert. Dress it up by serving in demitasse cups with espresso spoons, topped with a dollop of whipped cream and a meringue or sablé (page 37 or 40) for crunch.

makes 2½ cups or 8 generous servings

5 large egg yolks

½ cup sugar

⅓ cup water

8 ounces bittersweet chocolate (preferably 66% cacao), finely chopped

1 cup heavy cream, chilled

In the top of a double boiler or in a heat-proof bowl, whisk the yolks and sugar together until pale yellow and thick. A ribbon should fall back in the bowl when the whisk is lifted, and the sugar should begin to dissolve.

Stir in the water. Place over simmering water and cook, whisking vigorously, until the mixture is quite thick and coats the back of a spoon, about 160°F.

Remove from the heat and add the finely chopped chocolate. Stir until melted. Continue stirring until the mixture is cool to the touch.

In a separate bowl whisk the cream until soft peaks form. Gently fold into the melted chocolate mixture. Cover and refrigerate about 4 hours. Serve cold.

❊⁓{ chilled almond cream torte }⁓❊

If you love almonds as much as I do, this pure white-chocolate mousse studded with toasted almonds should become a regular for summer entertaining. It was inspired by my mother, who loved to finish a meal with something light and refreshing. This one is all about the play of textures—airy, creamy, cold mousse and crunchy toasted nuts. It's delightful with a Raspberry Sauce (page 175), berries, or brandied cherries (page 57).

serves 12 to 16

1½ cups (6 ounces) whole almonds

1 stick (8 tablespoons) unsalted butter, room temperature

½ cup sugar

¼ cup plus 2 tablespoons Amaretto

4 ounces white chocolate, finely chopped

2 cups heavy cream, chilled

½ cup additional toasted, chopped almonds for decorating (optional)

white-chocolate curls for decorating (page 14)

Line the bottom of a 9-inch round springform pan with a parchment circle and a 3-inch parchment strip around the inside edge.

Lightly toast the nuts in a 325°F oven for 10 to 13 minutes, until their fragrance is released. The almonds' interiors should be a light golden color when broken. Let cool.

Place the almonds in the food processor and pulse until the largest pieces are no more than ¼ inch. (Don't fret about uniformity.) Set aside.

In a mixer fitted with the paddle attachment, beat the butter and sugar on high speed until light and fluffy, 3 to 5 minutes. Add the Amaretto and mix well. Add the chopped almonds, beating until just combined. Set aside.

In a double boiler melt the chocolate over low heat. Remove the top of the boiler when the chocolate is nearly melted and continue stirring until smooth and glossy. Set aside to cool, stirring frequently until cool to the touch. (The finished temperature should be similar to the butter/almond mixture.) Return to the double boiler only briefly if it begins to set up.

In a separate bowl whisk the cold cream until soft peaks form. Chill in the refrigerator.

Stir the cooled melted chocolate into the almond mixture all at once. Lighten by quickly folding in one third of the cream. Gently fold in the remaining cream in 2 parts, trying not to overmix so the cream remains smooth and nearly liquid.

Evenly spread the mixture into the prepared pan and cover with plastic wrap. Place in the refrigerator or freezer to set at least 4 hours.

To serve, remove from the refrigerator or freezer. If frozen, let sit about 10 minutes to warm. Release and remove the sides of the springform pan. Remove the parchment strip. Turn the chilled torte over onto a serving plate. Release and remove the bottom of the pan and peel the parchment.

If desired, press additional, chopped toasted almonds onto the sides of the finished torte. Decorate the top with white chocolate curls. Store in the refrigerator and serve cold, cutting slices with a warm dry knife.

{ a simple bombe }

One of those super easy desserts that gives the impression that you worked much harder than you did, a bombe is simply layers of contrasting ice cream molded into a dome or a loaf. It is a wonderful, easy way to show off your scrumptious hand-churned ice creams since the cut slices turn into something quite beautiful and dramatic.

To make a bombe, choose a large domed bowl or loaf pan and fill with tap water. Pour the water into a glass measuring cup and use that volume measurement to determine the quantity of ice cream you will need. Dampen the bowl or pan with a moist paper towel, line with plastic wrap and place in the freezer for 20 minutes. Have ready two flavors of freshly churned ice cream or softened

store-bought. Almost Burnt Sugar (page 147) or Ginger Key Lime (page 148) would be spectacular with chocolate.

Using a spatula, spread one flavor of ice cream evenly over the bottom and sides of the mold. Freeze until firm, checking after 15 minutes for slumping. Build the sides back up if they do begin to slump. When the first layer is firm, spoon in the second flavor, filling the mold to the top. Smooth the top and cover with plastic wrap. Freeze until set. Before serving, invert to release and place the bombe on a serving platter. Peel the plastic and store in the freezer. Serve cold, cutting the slices with a warm, sharp knife. A dessert sauce or whipped cream is delicious as an accompaniment.

·} marquis au chocolat {·

The Marquis, a perfectly smooth, dense loaf of chilled bittersweet mousse, is a classic French restaurant dessert. An all-time favorite at Fran's retail stores, where it is often ordered for summer birthday celebrations, it's a great choice for the home cook throwing a big summer party. It cuts beautifully into very thin slices, can be made a day or two in advance, and there's no baking involved. The most important moment when making the Marquis is whipping the cream—it must be extremely loose to keep the texture lush. Serve with additional lightly whipped cream, Raspberry Sauce, or Crème Anglaise (page 100 or 175). Fresh berries would also be nice.   serves 12 to 16

5 large eggs, separated

½ cup plus 2 tablespoons sugar

½ cup water

8 ounces bittersweet chocolate, finely chopped

4 ounces unsweetened chocolate, finely chopped

1½ sticks (12 tablespoons) unsalted butter, room temperature

1 cup heavy cream, chilled

dark-chocolate curls for decorating (page 14)

Line the long sides and bottom of an 8½-by-4½-inch loaf pan with a single sheet of parchment paper measuring 8 by 14 inches. Then cut a 16-by-4-inch sheet of parchment and line the bottom and the short sides. There should be an excess of paper overhanging the pan in order to easily lift and remove the finished loaf.

In the top of a double boiler or heatproof bowl, whisk the yolks and ¼ cup sugar together until pale yellow and thick. A ribbon should fall back in the bowl when the whisk is lifted, and the sugar should begin to dissolve.

Stir in ¼ cup of the water. Place over simmering water and cook, whisking vigorously, until the mixture is quite thick and foamy, 160°F.

Remove from the heat and add the finely chopped chocolates. Stir until melted. Continue stirring until cool to the touch. Stir in the softened butter. Set aside.

In a separate bowl whisk the cream until soft peaks form. Chill in the refrigerator.

In a small heavy saucepan combine the remaining sugar (¼ cup plus 2 tablespoons) with the remaining ¼ cup water. Cook over medium heat, stirring until the sugar is dissolved and the mixture is clear. Increase the heat to high and boil, without stirring, until it thickens and large bubbles form, about a minute.

(continued)

Meanwhile, in the bowl of a mixer fitted with a clean whisk, begin whipping the egg whites on medium-high speed, increasing the speed until soft, glossy peaks form. With the mixer running, add the boiling sugar syrup in a slow, steady stream. Continue whipping until the peaks are stiff but not dry and the mixture feels tepid, about 90°F.

Lighten the cooled chocolate mixture by quickly folding in one-quarter of the beaten whites. Then gently fold in the remaining whites in 3 parts, trying not to overmix and lose the volume.

Repeat the folding process with the chilled whipped cream in 3 parts, gently folding until you can no longer see any streaks of white.

Evenly spread the mixture into the prepared pan, folding the excess parchment over the top. Cover with plastic wrap.

Place in refrigerator or freezer to set, about 4 hours.

Remove from the refrigerator or freezer. If frozen, let sit about 10 minutes to warm. Holding the flaps of parchment paper with both hands, gently lift the loaf from the pan. Invert onto a serving plate. Remove the parchment.

Store the Marquis in the refrigerator. Serve chilled, cutting with a warm dry knife. The flavors will get stronger as it warms up on the plate. Serve with lightly whipped cream.

white-chocolate espresso semifreddo

Installing freezer cases in our stores for the ice creams spurred me to develop a few special frozen desserts for feeding a crowd. This is one of the most popular and practical. It can keep for about two weeks in the freezer and is served in slices like a cake. Unlike most of my desserts, the taste of chocolate is subtle in this one—just the dark-chocolate crust, a dusting of cocoa, and a bit of white chocolate in the luscious whipped filling. The effect is like a tiramisu minus the ladyfingers.

serves 12 to 16

chocolate-wafer crust

ten 3¼-inch round Chocolate Wafers (page 39), or 1¾ cups cookie crumbs

1 tablespoon unsalted butter, melted

espresso mascarpone filling

½ cup espresso beans, finely ground

1 cup boiling water

4 large eggs, separated

⅓ cup plus 2 tablespoons sugar

1 tablespoon dark rum

2 teaspoons pure vanilla extract

4 ounces white chocolate, finely chopped

16 ounces mascarpone cheese

¼ cup heavy cream

¼ cup cold water

1 tablespoon Dutch-processed cocoa powder for decorating

to make the chocolate wafer crust

Position a rack in the middle of the oven and preheat the oven to 350°F. Lightly butter the bottom of a 9-inch round springform pan.

Crumble the chocolate wafers into a food processor fitted with the steel blade. Pulse until finely ground. Add the melted butter and pulse until blended. Or blend together crumbs and butter.

Press the crust evenly into the unlined, lightly coated pan. Bake for 10 minutes. When cool, line the sides with a 3-inch-wide parchment strip along the inside edge.

Place the finely ground espresso beans in a coffee filter over a glass measuring cup. Pour the boiling water over the grounds until coffee measures 3 ounces.

In the top of a double boiler or heatproof bowl, whisk together the yolks and 2 tablespoons of the sugar until pale yellow and thick. A ribbon should fall back in the bowl when the whisk is lifted and the sugar should begin to dissolve. Add the brewed espresso, rum, and vanilla. *(continued)*

Place over simmering water. Cook, vigorously whisking, until the liquid coats the back of a spoon (about 160°F) and the mixture is quite thick and foamy.

Remove from the heat and add the finely chopped white chocolate. Stir until melted. Continue stirring until the mixture is cool to the touch.

In a separate bowl, stir together the mascarpone and cream until soft and smooth. Cover with plastic and set aside in the refrigerator.

In a small heavy saucepan, stir together the remaining (⅓ cup) sugar with ¼ cup of cold water. Cook over medium heat, stirring until the sugar is dissolved and the mixture is clear. Increase the heat to high and boil, without stirring, until it thickens and large bubbles form, about 1 minute.

Meanwhile, in a bowl of a mixer fitted with a clean whisk, begin whipping the egg whites on medium-high speed, increasing the speed until soft, glossy peaks form. With the mixer running, add the boiling sugar syrup in a slow, steady stream.

Continue whipping until the peaks are stiff but not dry and the mixture feels tepid, about 90°F.

Remove the bowl from the mixer and all at once fold the chilled cream mixture into the white-chocolate mixture. Fold just until you no longer see any streaks of white. Lighten by quickly folding in one-quarter of the beaten whites. Then gently fold in the remaining whites in 3 parts, trying not to overmix and lose the volume.

Evenly spread the mixture over the baked crust in the pan. Using a fine-mesh sieve, dust the top with the cocoa powder. Cocoa powder will absorb moisture and become quite dark in color, deepening the cocoa flavor over time. Tightly cover with plastic wrap. Place in the freezer to set, at least 4 hours.

Loosen and remove the sides of the pan, removing any parchment. Store in the freezer and serve ice cold, cutting slices with a warm dry knife.

ᐧ{ triple-chocolate parfait }ᐧ

This triple-layer frozen dessert is like a cake with a secret agenda—the velvety, melt-in-your-mouth consistency of the richest ice cream. For the smoothest texture, just be sure to whip the cream very lightly. I like to serve this beautiful, totally chocolate showstopper directly from the freezer, before it begins melting and the flavors merge.   serves 16

Chocolate-Wafer Crust (page 39, 161), cooled

custard base

1 cup heavy cream

¼ cup plus 1 tablespoon whole milk

⅓ cup sugar

1 vanilla bean, split lengthwise

7 large egg yolks

dark-chocolate layer

5 ounces bittersweet chocolate, finely chopped

½ cup heavy cream, chilled

⅓ Custard Base recipe

2 tablespoons Kahlua

white-chocolate layer

⅓ Custard Base recipe

2 ounces white chocolate, finely chopped

½ cup heavy cream, chilled

1 tablespoon fine brandy or cognac

milk-chocolate layer

⅓ Custard Base recipe

7 ounces dark milk chocolate (preferably 42% cacao), finely chopped

½ cup heavy cream, chilled

Have ready the cooled Chocolate Wafer Crust.

to prepare the custard base

In a small, heavy saucepan, whisk together the cream, milk, and 1 teaspoon of the sugar. Using a paring knife, scrape the seeds of the vanilla bean into the mixture and toss in the bean. Cook over medium-low heat, stirring frequently, until it comes to a simmer. Remove from the heat.

In a mixing bowl whisk together the remaining sugar and the egg yolks. Slowly pour approximately one third of the warm cream mixture into the yolks, stirring constantly. Pour the yolk mixture back into the saucepan, stirring constantly.

Return to medium-low heat. Cook, stirring constantly, until the mixture begins to thicken and coats the back of a spoon, about 160°F. Remove from the heat.

(continued)

Remove and discard the vanilla bean. Evenly divide the base into 3 small mixing bowls. Cover the custards with plastic wrap touching the tops so a skin does not form. Refrigerate until cool but not cold.

to make the three chocolate layers

First make the Dark-Chocolate Layer. Melt the chocolate in a double boiler over low heat. Remove when nearly melted and continue stirring until smooth and glossy. Set aside to cool, stirring frequently. Return it to the double boiler only briefly if it begins to set up.

In a separate bowl whisk the cream until soft peaks form. Set aside in the refrigerator.

Remove one bowl of the Custard Base from the refrigerator and stir until smooth and creamy. There should be no lumps. Stir in the Kahlua. Fold the cooled, melted chocolate into the custard. Lighten by quickly folding in one-third of the whipped cream. Gently fold in the remaining cream in 2 parts.

to finish the parfait

Evenly spread the Dark-Chocolate Layer over the crust in the prepared pan. Cover with plastic wrap. Place in the freezer to set.

When the first layer is set, follow the same procedure to make the White-Chocolate Layer. Remove plastic wrap from dark layer. Spread white layer evenly over the dark layer, cover in plastic and freeze until set, about 20 minutes.

When the second layer is set, follow the same procedure to make the Milk-Chocolate Layer. Spread evenly over the white layer. Cover in plastic and freeze for at least 4 hours to set.

To serve, loosen and remove the sides of the pan. Remove the parchment. Serve ice cold, directly from the freezer, using a warm dry knife to cut.

·⟩ chocolate profiteroles ⟨·

Cream puffs are perfect receptacles for ice cream. These chocolate puffs stay extra dry thanks to the cocoa and the bottoms won't need to be scooped out. Now is no time to skimp on the sauce. Make some warm Pure Chocolate Sauce and revel in the contrast of temperatures and textures.   serves 6 to 8

¼ cup plus 3 tablespoons
all-purpose flour

2 tablespoons plus 1½ teaspoons
Dutch-processed cocoa powder

½ cup whole milk

½ stick (4 tablespoons) unsalted
butter

¾ teaspoon sugar

¼ teaspoon salt

2 large eggs

1 large egg white

2 pints favorite ice cream

Pure Chocolate Sauce (page 170)

Position a rack in the middle of the oven and preheat the oven to 425°F. Have ready 2 parchment- or Silpat-lined cookie sheets. Also have ready a large pastry bag fitted with a large round pastry tip (#808) about ⅝ inch in diameter.

Sift together the flour and cocoa 3 times. Set aside.

In a small heavy saucepan over medium-high heat, bring the milk, butter, sugar, and salt to a boil. Reduce heat to medium. Add the flour mixture all at once, whisking constantly to remove all lumps. Then switch to a wooden spoon and continue stirring over medium heat until the dough forms a ball. It should begin slightly sticking to the bottom of the pan.

Transfer to a bowl of a mixer fitted with a paddle attachment. Begin mixing on medium speed. Add the eggs and egg white, one at a time, beating well between each addition. Beat until the mixture is smooth, glossy, and slightly warm to the touch, stopping several times to scrape down the sides of the bowl.

Transfer the dough to a pastry bag. Pipe 24 to 30 round domes, about 1½ inches in diameter, onto the lined cookie sheets. (Or use a small ice-cream scoop.)

Bake for 15 minutes. Then lower the temperature to 350°F and bake an additional 10 to 15 minutes. Set aside to cool. The finished profiteroles should be crisp and puffy. As they cool, they will soften a bit.

To serve, with a sharp knife split the profiteroles across the width. Fill each bottom with a small scoop of ice cream, replacing the tops to completely cover the ice cream. Place 3 profiteroles on each plate, forming a triangle. Top with a fourth, spoon on sauce, and serve.

{ silken dessert sauces }

⁙{ pure chocolate sauce }⁙

When I was growing up, we always kept two kinds of Hershey's chocolate sauce in the house—the thick fudgey one and the thin syrup. I much preferred the thicker kind, spooned out of the can and warmed up for my ice-cream sundaes.

This grown-up version of that fudgey, warm sauce is a tad more luxurious. It is so easy to make and such a delight to eat—like licking a warm, liquid truffle—that it belongs in your pantry at all times, for instant sundae making whenever the mood strikes. Celebrate being an adult by adding a splash of your favorite liqueur to the melted chocolate.

makes 1½ cups

1 cup heavy cream

8 ounces bittersweet chocolate, finely chopped

In a small saucepan bring the cream just to a boil. Remove from the heat and add the chopped chocolate. Let set one minute. Stir with a heatproof rubber spatula until smooth. Set aside to cool slightly. Serve warm or store in a sealed container in the refrigerator.

To reheat, place the container in a pot of warm water until the sauce is warm and loose.

⁕} chocolate espresso sauce {⁕

Seattle's weather demands great coffee—and we have the best chocolate!
In this wonderfully simple dairy-free sauce, the aroma of espresso lends
an elegant edge. Serve over small scoops of ice cream or profiteroles for
complete after-dinner bliss.

makes 1¼ cups

8 ounces bittersweet chocolate,
finely chopped

½ cup plus 2 tablespoons brewed
espresso or triple-strength coffee,
room temperature

In a double boiler melt the chocolate over
low heat. Remove the top of the boiler
when the chocolate is nearly melted and
stir until glossy and smooth. Add the
espresso all at once and whisk until the
sauce is completely smooth. Set aside to
cool slightly.

Serve warm or store in a sealed container
in the refrigerator. Reheat gently to serve.

deepest, darkest chocolate sauce

This intensely dark sauce has great depth of flavor and sheen. I use it as the finishing touch on all sorts of desserts from cakes to mousses, and it is my standard syrup for beverage making. A few spoonfuls lend great flavor to sodas, milkshakes, and hot mochas. You can pour it over ice cream as well.

makes 1½ cups

1 cup heavy cream

¾ cup sugar

½ cup corn syrup

¾ cup Dutch-processed cocoa powder, sifted into a mixing bowl

In a heavy saucepan stir together the cream and sugar. Cook over medium heat, stirring occasionally, until the sugar dissolves. Stir in the corn syrup and bring to a boil.

Remove from the heat and pour half of the mixture into the mixing bowl with the sifted cocoa. Whisk by hand until smooth. Then add the remaining warm cream and continue whisking until smooth.

Pour through a fine-mesh sieve back into the saucepan. Place over low heat and slowly cook until large bubbles form and the surface is glossy, about 5 minutes. Remove from the heat and set aside to cool slightly. Serve warm, or store in a sealed container in the refrigerator as long as 2 weeks.

❧{ crème anglaise }☙

The classic, cool white sauce for puddling beneath a slice of chocolate torte,
Marquis au Chocolat (page 158), or any of the mousses or ice creams.

makes about 3¼ cups, enough for 12 servings

2½ cups whole milk

½ cup plus 2 tablespoons sugar

6 large egg yolks

1 teaspoon cornstarch

1½ teaspoons pure vanilla extract

In a heavy saucepan whisk together the
milk and 2 tablespoons of the sugar. Cook
over medium-low heat, stirring frequently
until the milk comes to a simmer. Remove
from the heat.

In a mixing bowl, whisk together the
remaining sugar, egg yolks, and cornstarch. Slowly pour approximately one
third of the warm milk into the yolk mixture, stirring constantly. Pour the yolk
mixture back into the saucepan, continu-
ing to stir.

Return to the heat. Cook, stirring constantly, until the mixture begins to thicken
and coats the back of a spoon, about
160°F. Remove from the heat. Strain
through a fine-mesh sieve. Stir in the
vanilla.

Cover with plastic wrap touching the top
so a skin does not form. Refrigerate for as
long as 5 days and serve chilled.

VARIATION

*For Chocolate Crème Anglaise, after the
custard has thickened, remove from the heat.
Add 6 ounces finely chopped semisweet or
bittersweet chocolate and stir until smooth.
Strain and chill. Serve with the Marquis
(page 158) or with the Belgian-Chocolate
Cheesecake (page 130).*

❈} raspberry sauce {❈

Few flavors go as well as raspberries with dark- and white-chocolate desserts. It provides the perfect bright red color and tart contrast for luxuries like Brie White-Chocolate Cheesecake (page 133), Marquis au Chocolat (page 158), and Chocolate Espresso Torte (page 71). I'm sure you won't run out of uses for it.

Lightly cooking the raspberries concentrates their flavor and gives the sauce better keeping powers than an uncooked sauce. At the height of the season, I like to make batches and freeze them for all my winter dessert making.   makes 1½ cups, enough for 16 servings

2 pints fresh raspberries or
1 pound thawed frozen, with juices
reserved

⅔ cup plus 2 tablespoons sugar

1 tablespoon lemon juice

In a saucepan combine all of the ingredients. Bring to a simmer and cook over low heat until the sauce thickens, about 10 minutes. Stir often to avoid scorching. Strain through a fine-mesh sieve. Set aside to cool.

Store in a sealed jar in the refrigerator for as long as 2 weeks, or freeze.

⋅⋅{ milk-chocolate sauce }⋅⋅

A thin, fine milk-chocolate sauce such as this complements an intensely dark-chocolate dessert without overwhelming it. Choose a high-cacao-content milk chocolate for the best flavor.

makes 1¾ cups

1¼ cups heavy cream or milk

11 ounces dark milk chocolate (preferably 42–46% cacao), finely chopped

In a small saucepan bring the cream to a simmer. Remove from the heat and add the chocolate. Stir with a rubber spatula until smooth. Serve or store in a sealed container in the refrigerator. Gently reheat to serve.

❋} caramel sauce {❋

As you develop your confidence working with sugar, you'll learn the exact right moment to take it off the heat for perfect caramel flavor. Don't fret if you overcook your caramel when you're learning how. Just try again. As someone who has cooked a lot of sugar in her day, I can tell you that the trick to developing depth of flavor and complexity is slow cooking.

To test caramel for thickness, spoon some on a saucer and let it cool. Then run a finger through the puddle of sauce. The finger's pathway should hold a channel for about 5 seconds before the walls start collapsing. If the sauce is too thick, you can thin it by stirring in more cream.   makes a scant 2 cups

2½ cups sugar

½ cup water

1½ cups heavy cream

In a medium saucepan combine the sugar and water. Cook over medium heat, stirring occasionally, until the sugar is dissolved and the mixture is clear. Increase the heat to high and bring to a boil. Cook without stirring until the mixture turns a light golden brown, about 10 minutes. Occasionally brush down the sides of the pan with a pastry brush dipped in water.

When the mixture begins to caramelize around the edges and has the distinct, nutty fragrance of caramel, lift the pan and gently swirl for even browning.

Remove from the heat and slowly pour in the cream, continuously stirring with a long-handled wooden spoon. Don't worry about the sugar bubbling up as steam escapes. It bubbles a good long time and then it will stop. Keep stirring until smooth. Let cool about 15 minutes.

Serve warm or store in a sealed container in the refrigerator for as long as 2 weeks. Gently reheat to serve.

⁑❳ chocolate caramel sauce ❲⁑

This is a wonderful marriage of my two favorites, chocolate and caramel. The caramelization adds depth to the sugar, and the chocolate finishes it with great flavor. Take care to select a chocolate that is bittersweet enough for your tastes, such as a 70 percent cacao Valrhona or Scharffen Berger.

makes 3 cups

2½ cups sugar

½ cup water

1½ cups heavy cream

4 ounces bittersweet chocolate, finely chopped

In a medium saucepan combine the sugar and water. Cook over low heat until the sugar is dissolved and the mixture is clear.

Increase the heat to high and bring to a boil. Cook, without stirring, until light golden brown, about 10 minutes. Have nearby a cup of water and a pastry brush for brushing down the sugar crystals that form on the sides of the pan. Once the color starts changing you want to watch carefully, since caramel can burn quickly. When dark golden brown, lift the pan and gently swirl for even browning.

Remove from the heat and slowly pour in the cream, continuously stirring with a long-handled wooden spoon. Don't worry about the sugar bubbling up as steam escapes. It bubbles a good long time, and then it will stop. Keep stirring until smooth. Let cool 5 minutes.

Stir in the chopped chocolate until smooth. Serve warm or store in a sealed container in the refrigerator. Reheat gently to serve.

⁕{ five beverages and a snack }⁕

❧ hot chocolate ☙

Hot chocolate as it was meant to be! The hot milk releases the flavor and sensuality of cocoa butter so the experience is like drinking a warm truffle. If you've shopped at my stores, you know that we sell shaved chocolate in canisters for those who are too time crunched in the morning for grating. Everyone deserves their daily chocolate!

serves 1

¾ cup milk

2 ounces semi- or bittersweet chocolate, thinly shaved or grated

In a small saucepan bring the milk to a simmer. Remove from the heat and stir in the chocolate until completely smooth. It takes about 1 minute for maximum smoothness. Pour into a serving cup and enjoy.

❧ pure hot chocolate ☙

For the purist, fine chocolate mixed with only water reveals the nuances of the chocolate itself. This is an excellent way to do a chocolate tasting. Chop up a few different kinds of chocolate, mix with hot water, and pour into espresso cups for thoughtful sipping.

serves 1

¾ cup water

2 ounces semi- or bittersweet chocolate, thinly shaved or grated

In a small saucepan bring the water just to a simmer over medium heat. Remove from the heat, add the chocolate, and whisk until smooth. Pour into a serving cup and enjoy.

⋅⋅{ hot cocoa }⋅⋅

As for most of us, cocoa was my very first chocolate beverage. I have fond memories of my grandmother Frances Hazel, whom I called Grandma Mom, warming the milk while I made a serious job of stirring the paste in the cup.

If you have ever pondered the terminology, hot cocoa is always made from cocoa powder and hot chocolate from chocolate.

serves 1

1 tablespoon Dutch-processed cocoa powder

1 tablespoon sugar

2 tablespoons cream

½ cup hot milk

Select your favorite mug or teacup. In the bottom, mix the cocoa powder, sugar, and cream with a spoon to form a paste. Pour in the hot milk and stir until smooth and thoroughly combined.

chocolate milk shake

Today's milk shakes are never quite as cold and thick as those I remember pouring from the frosty silver canisters at the Creamland Ice Creamery. Wimpy modern milk shakes begin with soft serve—a serious sacrilege as far as I'm concerned. The trick to a great old-fashioned shake is to start with hard, ice-cold ice cream. You can get more chocolate flavor by substituting chocolate ice cream, or make it mocha by substituting a shot of espresso for the milk. Get out your long-handled spoons and enjoy!

serves 1

3 tablespoons Deepest, Darkest Chocolate Sauce (page 172)

2½ scoops best-quality vanilla ice cream, frozen hard

⅓ cup cold milk

In a blender, combine the chocolate sauce, ½ scoop of the ice cream, and milk. Purée on low speed until blended. Add the remaining ice cream and blend on low speed to combine, less than a minute. Pour into a tall, chilled glass and enjoy.

❧ chocolate soda ❧

I learned my soda-making techniques at my first job, at the Creamland Ice Creamery in the Greenwood neighborhood of Seattle. At this gleaming soda fountain of the fifties, I spent my summer weekends mastering the art of sodas, sundaes, milkshakes—the works. What a dream job!

This classic soda remains a great summertime refresher. If you feel like branching out, try substituting coffee ice cream, or combine Caramel Sauce (page 177) with chocolate ice cream, or Raspberry Sauce (page 175) with vanilla ice cream or raspberry sorbet. The sky's the limit!

serves 1

3 tablespoons Deepest, Darkest Chocolate Sauce (page 172), or prepared

3 scoops best-quality vanilla ice cream (1 scoop softened)

Plain sparkling or carbonated water

In a tall glass, mix the chocolate sauce and 1 scoop of softened ice cream with a spoon to make a paste. Pour in sparkling water until the glass is half full and mix.

Add the remaining 2 scoops of hard ice cream until the soda level is 1 inch from the rim. Drizzle in additional sparkling water from 3 inches above the glass for those soda-fountain bubbles.

·:} bread and chocolate {:·

When I shared my latest secret breakfast with my son, Dylan, he told me he'd been indulging for years. Like an instant *pain au chocolat* straight out of the oven, the warmth of the toast releases chocolate's fragrance for all your senses to enjoy. The interplay of earthy wheat and unctuous cacao is pure and simple magic.

serves 1

one ½-inch-thick slice rustic artisan-style bread

1½ to 2 tablespoons (¼ ounce) shaved or grated bittersweet chocolate

Toast your bread. While still warm, sprinkle the chocolate over the surface, and watch it melt and turn into a sumptuous treat.

{ truffles and other fine chocolates }

TEMPERING DARK CHOCOLATE

If you're one of those folks who thinks life is too short to stuff cherry tomatoes, you may not have the patience for tempering chocolate. If, on the other hand, you get a secret shiver every time your puff pastry rises, tempering chocolate could be deeply satisfying. All it takes is time and devotion. And about two pounds of chocolate—any less will hinder your chances of success.

Tempering is the process of melting, cooling, and melting chocolate again to realign the crystals in the cocoa butter. The resulting chocolate is perfectly smooth and shiny and snaps cleanly when broken. It is the chocolate used by professionals for coating fine candies and fruits and molding whimsical shapes. I consider it totally optional for home cooks, though it is the fine line that signals professional-level candies. All of the truffles and bites that follow are delicious without a tempered coating. That glossy shell is simply the finishing touch.

To temper chocolate, three key elements have to come together seamlessly: time, temperature, and movement. You'll increase your odds of success by beginning with freshly opened bars of high-quality semisweet chocolate, already in temper when they leave the factory. The higher-percentage chocolates are more temperamental and take more experience.

In addition to a cool kitchen (about 68 degrees), you will need a reliable thermometer and about two hours' uninterrupted time to devote to pampering your chocolate. It is essential to read the recipe through first and, most important, to have ready your centers and other delectable morsels for dipping before you begin tempering. The pieces should be at room temperature.

One thing I've noticed in my classes is that beginners have a greater chance of success if they can turn the whole tempering and dipping process into a social occasion, so it isn't so deadly serious. One faithful student returns every year to purchase thirty pounds of chocolate for her annual holiday candy-making extravaganza. At the end of the dipping instructions you will find several quick candy ideas for using up that well-tempered chocolate with helpful family and friends.

tempering dark chocolate

2 pounds high-quality semisweet chocolate (preferably 56% cacao), finely chopped (enough to dip about 100 candy centers)

Reserve 7 ounces of the finely chopped chocolate.

Place the remaining chopped chocolate in a large stainless-steel bowl over simmering water or in a double boiler over low heat.

When about half of the chocolate is melted, remove from the heat. Stir with a dry, heatproof spatula until smooth. Return to the heat and continue stirring until the chocolate reaches 115°F. Do not let the temperature exceed 120°F.

Remove from the heat and add the reserved 7 ounces of finely chopped chocolate. Stir with the spatula until all the chocolate is melted and smooth.

Continue stirring every few minutes until the chocolate cools to a temperature of 82–84°F. Depending on the temperature of your kitchen and the size of your bowl, this may take anywhere from 15 to 30 minutes. Patience is a virtue.

Once the chocolate is cool, return over simmering water very briefly to gently warm back to 88 to 90°F. This crucial step takes 10 seconds at most. If the chocolate goes over 90 degrees, it is likely to lose its temper and you will need to start the process over from the beginning. Be vigilant and keep the water at the barest simmer.

The perfect temperature for fluid dark chocolate for dipping is between 88 and 90°F. To test for temper, smear a teaspoonful on a sheet of parchment or a plate. If it dries within 2 minutes to a glossy, smooth finish, it is in temper. If it doesn't set properly and looks dull and streaked, it probably needs more time to cool. Continue stirring and testing. Once the chocolate is in temper, have your pieces ready for dipping and work quickly.

If the chocolate starts to firm around the edges, briefly return the bowl to simmering water to keep it fluid enough for dipping—but not above 90°F.

Leftover tempered chocolate is best used for baking or dessert making. Simply pour onto a parchment-lined sheet to harden. Then break into chunks and store with your baking chocolate.

In dipping the centers you will keep one hand clean and use one hand for dipping in the chocolate. Using your clean hand, drop a center into the tempered chocolate. With your other hand, retrieve the submerged center, using your index and middle fingers. Make sure the center is evenly coated on all surfaces and edges. Slightly separate your two fingers, lift the center and gently shake the excess chocolate back into the bowl. Carefully place the chocolate on a parchment or Silpat-lined sheet pan to set, 5 to 8 minutes, at room temperature.

Or using a dipping or dinner fork, lift out the coated centers. Shake off the excess chocolate and gently place on a lined sheet pan or Silpat. As you gain experience, the tines of the fork can be used to decorate the tops. While the chocolate is still wet, press and lift the tines to leave lines.

For a rougher, less-polished finish, tumble the dipped centers back and forth between the fingers of your hand.

to decorate dipped chocolates

Coating freshly dipped chocolates in nuts or cocoa is an excellent way to mask any imperfections, emphasize a flavor, and add crunch. Put cocoa or finely chopped toasted almonds, pistachios, or hazelnuts in a small bowl. Drop each freshly dipped chocolate in the bowl to coat. Wait 5 to 10 seconds, then roll to completely cover. Let set 2 to 3 minutes and transfer to a sheet pan to set.

quick treats with tempered chocolate

Now that you've achieved perfectly tempered chocolate, we don't want any of that bright, shiny chocolate to go to waste. Here are a few quick ideas for unfussy treats you can toss together after your centers have all been beautifully coated.

Fruits dipped in tempered chocolate have better chocolate flavor, brighter sheen, and a cleaner snap than those coated with a combination of chocolate and oil or shortening. Don't forget that plain cookies like shortbreads, meringues, and biscotti dipped in chocolate are always a treat!

CHOCOLATE-DIPPED CHERRIES

Bing or Rainier cherries are both delicious, though I am partial to Rainiers. Their tartness is perfect with chocolate. Wash the cherries with the stems on and remove the pit with a cherry pitter or small knife. Let completely dry. Holding the stems, dip cherries in the tempered chocolate and transfer to parchment paper to set. Dipped cherries can keep for 2 days.

CHOCOLATE-DIPPED STRAWBERRIES

Clean strawberries and pat dry, leaving the husks and stems on. Partially dip the berries in the warm tempered chocolate and place on parchment paper to set. Dipped strawberries should be served the same day.

(continued)

the secret of the centers

*t*raditionally, the moment a hand-dipped chocolate is pulled out of its chocolate bath, the maker quickly drizzles wet chocolate along the top, leaving a "sign" or a clue to the flavor within. Boxes of my candies do come with a little map, or key to the signs, to eliminate surprises. Fran's cognoscenti should know that our first truffle, the Dark Chocolate, is marked with a V—my personal homage to Frederick & Nelson's Victorian creams, one of my childhood favorites. After the V was taken, we started marking candies consecutively as they were added to the line: one line for Grand Marnier, two for Kahlua and three for praline. To make life easier for the caffeine lovers, we chose E for espresso and for no apparent reason the Irish Whiskey is drizzled with white chocolate. Each maker invents her own secret code.

DRIED FRUIT MENDIANTS

Mendiants are traditional European medallions of fine chocolate studded with a selection of nuts and dried fruits. Easy and sophisticated, they are a wonderful addition to a candy tray. I like to explore the bulk bins at the natural foods market for new items like cranberries and sour cherries in addition to old favorites like plump, moist figs and apricots. Other possibilities are candied orange and lemon peel and candied ginger. Cut the dried fruits and peels into small pieces, no larger than 1/4 inch.

Gather an assortment of nuts such as almonds, hazelnuts, pistachios, walnuts, and pecans, all toasted and cooled. Depending on size, small nuts can be used whole, walnuts and pecans in halves and almonds in slivers. Have your fruit and nuts ready.

Drop a spoonful of warm tempered chocolate onto a parchment-lined sheet pan, forming a 2-inch round disk. Quickly arrange an assortment of dried fruits and nuts in an attractive pattern on the chocolate. Each disc should hold 2 different nut pieces and at least 4 or 5 small pieces of fruit. Let set at room temperature. Store in a cool dry place for up to 3 weeks.

FRESH BERRY MENDIANTS

These are fantastic in the summer when raspberries and blueberries are at their peak. Following the method for dried fruit, form slightly smaller disks of tempered chocolate, about 1 1/2-inch rounds. Top with 3 to 5 clean, dry berries and let set. Fresh berries are fragile and best eaten the same day. Invite a crowd.

CHOCOLATE NUT CLUSTERS

In a bowl, combine equal amounts tempered chocolate and cooled, toasted nuts. Whole macadamias, almonds, and hazelnuts are fantastic. Gently stir together and then drop by spoonfuls onto a parchment-lined sheet to set.

}how to taste a truffle{

The truffles I prefer are small, no more than two or three bites. When I first started out as a chocolatier, Americans favored super-size bonbons, but now, with more appreciation for intense flavors, I think the tide is changing. Eating fine chocolate deserves your serious attention. Here are recommendations for total truffle-eating pleasure from someone for whom tasting truffles is all in a day's work.

The first bite is all about snap and anticipation. Listen to the crisp shell break as the smooth creamy center is released into your mouth. Enjoy the contrasting textures and the first hint of flavor just under your nose. As the chocolate melts, the scent creates nuances of flavor. As you swallow, fine chocolate is warmed by body heat, coating your mouth and creating that sensuous "mouthfeel" that pulls us back for more.

❧ pure dark-chocolate truffles ❧

Here is the truffle that started it all. Back in 1982, when I thought I was opening a pastry shop, I placed about 200 cocoa-dusted dark truffles on the counter for those who might want a quick bite while selecting their evening's dessert. Within three months, the message was clear. People in Seattle needed more chocolate. In the time-honored tradition of small-business owners, I trained on the job. I experimented with liqueurs (starting out with naturals like Kahlua and Grand Marnier), took lessons in the lost art of hand-dipping from a local cooking teacher, and fiddled with my chocolate and cream until the magic of time, temperature, and movement arrived at my fingertips like second nature.

I soon learned that a perfectly smooth consistency, without a grain, is what sets extraordinary truffles apart. And few combinations are more perfect than cream and chocolate. This is the truffle I continue to return to whenever I discover an extraordinary new chocolate and want to highlight its taste. As you set off on your own chocolate-making adventures, you'll want to start out with a favorite chocolate and pay careful attention to how the cream transforms that sensuous ingredient into something much more.

makes 50 to 60 pieces

12 ounces semisweet chocolate, finely chopped

1 cup heavy cream

3 tablespoons unsalted butter, room temperature

1 recipe tempered semisweet chocolate (page 193) (optional)

Place the finely chopped chocolate in a large mixing bowl and set aside.

In a small pot bring the cream to a boil. Pour over the chocolate in the bowl. Let sit approximately 30 seconds without disturbing.

With a rubber spatula, beginning in a small area in the middle of the bowl, start stirring with small, gentle strokes. As the puddle in the center turns dark and smooth, begin making broader strokes, moving out to the edges and gradually incorporating more of the cream and chocolate. Continue stirring until the mixture is smooth and dark. The emulsion should be very smooth.

(continued)

Cover with plastic wrap touching the surface of the ganache. Let set at room temperature 8 to 12 hours or overnight, allowing the flavors to develop and the consistency to firm up.

to form the truffles

Have ready two 9-by-13-inch or quarter-sheet pans, or a half-sheet pan lined with parchment.

To form the centers, the butter must be soft enough to blend easily with a spatula. (If the butter is hard, let sit longer or beat with the paddle attachment on a mixer to soften.) Place the softened butter in a bowl and beat with a rubber spatula until the consistency is similar to the chocolate ganache.

With the rubber spatula, fold the butter into the ganache until smooth, glossy, and homogeneous. The mixture is ready when it mounds in the bowl and holds a shape when piped. (If it firms up too much, gently warm for 5 seconds over barely simmering water, just to soften the edges.)

Spoon into a pastry bag fitted with a ½-inch round tip (#806). Pipe fifty to sixty 1-inch rounds onto the lined sheets. Transfer to the refrigerator for at least 1 hour to firm up.

If you're uncomfortable with a pastry bag, a small scoop or teaspoon can be used to portion out the centers. If using the scoop method, let centers set in the refrigerator just until firm enough to roll by hand into balls, about 20 minutes.

When set, trim the tails on top of the chocolates by holding each in one hand and cutting with a small paring knife to form a smooth top. (Or remove the tails earlier, before the chocolate has set, by gently running a finger across the top.) Replace on sheet. Let the trimmed centers come to room temperature.

Following the tempering and dipping instructions (page 193), dip pieces in dark chocolate.

Store at cool room temperature; 68–72°F is ideal.

VARIATIONS

COCOA-DUSTED TRUFFLES

If tempering is not your cup of tea, dark-chocolate truffles are marvelous just dusted with cocoa in the traditional French manner. Simply roll the trimmed centers in a bowl of dark cocoa powder. Store in the refrigerator. Fragile cocoa-dusted truffles are best eaten within 3 days.

CHAMBORD TRUFFLES

Prepare a ganache following the Pure Dark Chocolate Truffles recipe, substituting 13 ounces chocolate and 1 cup heavy cream. Once it is a smooth emulsion, stir in 3 tablespoons Chambord (black raspberry) liqueur and continue with the recipe.

Other spirits that make a good match with chocolate are Kahlua, Amaretto, Grand Marnier, Irish Whiskey, Cognac, and dark rum.

espresso bites

The best method for adding flavor to a truffle is to first infuse the cream as we do in this classic pairing of coffee and chocolate. The same procedure can be used for adding the taste of vanilla bean, herbs, teas, or cinnamon sticks to a chocolate center.

All of the poured chocolates or "bites" that follow can be piped or scooped to form traditional round truffles by referring to the method for Pure Dark-Chocolate Truffles (page 197). I devised this pouring method to eliminate errors for beginning chocolate makers.

makes about 96 pieces

26 ounces semisweet chocolate, finely chopped

3 cups heavy cream

¾ cup crushed espresso beans

¾ stick (6 tablespoons) unsalted butter, room temperature

1 recipe tempered semisweet chocolate (page 193) (optional)

Have ready a 9-by-13-inch or quarter-sheet pan lined with parchment.

Place the finely chopped chocolate in a bowl and set aside.

In a saucepan, heat the cream and the crushed espresso beans on medium-high heat just until the cream begins to boil. Remove from the heat and let steep for 15 minutes to infuse. Strain into a measuring cup to remove the beans. You should have 2 cups of cream. If short, add additional cream to the 2-cup measure.

Return the infused cream to the heat and bring back to a boil. Remove from the heat and pour over the chocolate in the bowl. Let sit approximately 30 seconds without disturbing.

With a rubber spatula, beginning in a small area in the middle of the bowl, start stirring in small, gentle strokes. As the puddle in the center turns dark and smooth, begin making broader strokes, moving out to the edges and gradually incorporating more of the cream and chocolate. Continue stirring until the mixture is smooth and dark. The emulsion should be very smooth.

Let the mixture cool about 40 minutes, stirring every 10 minutes until it begins to mound on the surface but settles back into the mixture within 20 seconds. You do not want to incorporate any air, just start the setting process.

Before adding the butter, check that it is the same consistency as the ganache. If too hard, beat it to soften. Stir the softened butter into the chocolate until no traces remain. Pour the ganache into the prepared pan, spreading evenly with an offset metal spatula.

Let set, uncovered, until firm to the touch, at least 8 to 12 hours at room temperature, but no longer than 24 hours.

To remove, run a thin knife around the pan to loosen. Turn out onto a cutting board and remove the parchment. Using a long thin blade, cut the ganache into 8 strips lengthwise and 12 strips across the width, to make bite-size pieces.

Arrange on a parchment-lined pan and allow to set until firm to the touch, up to 12 hours. If storing the chocolates longer (up to 24 hours), cover with an inverted sheet pan. If you choose not to dip, the cut pieces can be tossed in dark-cocoa powder or left plain and set in little paper or foil cups.

If desired, following the tempering and dipping instructions, dip the pieces in dark chocolate.

the art of hand dipping

My very first truffles at the shop were simply handmade centers of dark-chocolate ganache coated with dark cocoa. Without a hard shell to protect them, they were luxuriously soft and smooth in the mouth—what a French housewife might make for her family—but thoroughly impractical in a retail environment. They had absolutely no shelf life and wouldn't hold a shape for long without refrigeration. It quickly became apparent that if I wanted my chocolates to last longer than a day or two, I would have to protect them with a crisp shell of chocolate. I set my sights on a very thin, hand-dipped shell.

Hand dipping is a vanishing American tradition. After asking around Seattle's food community, I found a woman in town who could pass along the fine art of chocolate dipping.

Judith St. Hilaire had spent years becoming a master candy-dipper, and her technique was perfection. The meditative quality of sitting in front of a vat of warm chocolate all day suited her well, and she was a marvelous teacher. Working alongside Judith and copying her long, graceful strokes, I learned how to dip a center just long enough to pull it out, shake off the excess, and plop it on a tray. She taught me how to make those little lines on top called "signs" that I remembered so fondly from my childhood forays to the candy counter at Frederick & Nelson's—the signs that reveal the secrets of the centers.

❧ orange bites ❧

A perennial favorite at Fran's, this Grand Marnier truffle combines tart fragrant orange oil with bitter chocolate—a combination that always has its loyal fans. The common thread that all of the great chocolate accents share is they are distinctive enough to complement chocolate's richness without overwhelming its flavor. Other time-honored classics are vanilla, cinnamon, coffee, almonds, and hazelnuts.

makes about 96 pieces

26 ounces semisweet chocolate, finely chopped

2 cups heavy cream

2 oranges

2 tablespoons Grand Marnier

½ stick (4 tablespoons) unsalted butter, room temperature

1 recipe tempered semisweet chocolate (page 193) (optional)

Have ready a 9-by-13-inch or quarter-sheet pan lined with parchment.

Place the finely chopped chocolate in a bowl and set aside.

Pour the cream into a saucepan. Holding a microplaner over the saucepan, zest only the darkest part of the orange skins into the cream, making sure to catch all of the orange oil. Heat over medium-high heat just until the cream begins to boil. Remove from the heat, and let steep for 10 minutes to infuse.

Return to the heat and bring back to the boil. Remove from the heat and pour over the chocolate in the bowl. Let sit approximately 30 seconds without disturbing.

With a rubber spatula, beginning in a small area in the middle of the bowl, start stirring in small, gentle strokes. As the puddle in the center turns dark and smooth, begin making broader strokes, moving out to the edges and gradually incorporating more of the cream and chocolate. Continue stirring until the mixture is smooth and dark. The emulsion should be very smooth.

Gently stir in the Grand Marnier.

Let the mixture cool for about 40 minutes, stirring every 10 minutes until it begins to mound on the surface, but settles back into the mixture within 20 seconds.

Before adding the butter, check that it is the same consistency as the ganache. If it is too hard, beat it to soften. Stir the softened butter into the chocolate until no traces remain.

Pour the ganache into the prepared pan, spreading it evenly with an offset metal spatula. Let the ganache set, uncovered, a minimum of 8 to 12 hours at room temperature, until firm to the touch. Do not let it set longer than 24 hours.

To remove, run a thin knife around the pan to loosen. Turn out onto a cutting board and remove the parchment. Using a thin blade, cut the ganache into 8 strips lengthwise and 12 strips across the width, to make bite-size pieces.

Arrange pieces on a parchment-lined pan and allow to set until firm to the touch, up to 12 hours. If storing the chocolates longer (up to 24 hours), cover with an inverted sheet pan. If you choose not to dip, the cut pieces can be tossed in dark-cocoa powder or left plain and placed in little paper or foil cups.

If desired, following the tempering and dipping instructions, dip the pieces in dark chocolate.

VARIATION

For Lemon Chocolates, substitute lemons for the oranges and omit the Grand Marnier.

❖{ boule d'amande }❖

These elegant milk-chocolate spheres have it all: a creamy milk-chocolate center, a crisp dark chocolate shell, and a crunchy coating of toasted nuts. They are a wonderful choice for the beginning candy maker. Milk chocolate is much easier to work with than dark chocolate, almost everyone loves it, and you have the added bonus of toasted almonds covering any imperfections in the dipping. (Let's not forget that milk chocolate and almonds are one of the classic childhood candy bars.) Boules have the highest success rate of all the candies in my holiday classes. Make sure to scoop small enough centers since the little balls keep growing as they take on their coatings.   makes 60 to 70 pieces

1 cup heavy cream

1 pound milk chocolate (preferably 36–46% cacao), finely chopped

1 recipe tempered semisweet chocolate (page 193) (optional)

3 cups whole almonds, toasted and finely chopped (page 19)

Have ready two 9-by-13-inch or quarter-sheet pans or 1 half-sheet pan lined with parchment.

In a saucepan, heat the cream over medium-high heat just until it begins to boil. Remove from the heat. Add the finely chopped milk chocolate. Using a rubber spatula, stir until smooth.

Pour the mixture into a bowl. Cover with plastic wrap touching the top and let set at room temperature for 6 to 8 hours, until firm enough to scoop or pipe.

When the ganache is set, gently stir a few times with a rubber spatula. Spoon into a pastry bag fitted with a ½-inch round tip (#806). Pipe round balls, about ¾ inch in diameter, onto a parchment-lined pan. (You can also use a melon baller or small scoop to form the centers.) Let set at room temperature until firm to the touch, about 2 hours.

Then gently roll the balls in the palms of your hands to round out their shape. (If you choose not to dip in tempered chocolate, roll in chopped almonds to coat.) Place balls back on the parchment-lined pan. Let set until firm to the touch, about 2 hours.

When ready to dip, spread the chopped almonds on a sheet pan.

Dip each chocolate ball in tempered chocolate to coat evenly, shaking off the excess. Then immediately drop each chocolate in the nuts. Wait 5 to 10 seconds, then roll to completely cover. Let set 2 to 3 minutes, transfer to a parchment-lined sheet, and let set.

Stored between 60 and 68 degrees, the chocolates can be kept up to 2 weeks.

❧ chocolate fondue ❧

Fondue turns dessert into an interactive event. There's just something primal about allowing people to control their own dessert. Kids of all ages love spearing their pieces and getting as much chocolate as possible onto their fruit or any other available surfaces. So hide your finest tablecloth and be prepared to get messy.

To avoid traffic jams around the fondue pot, I sometimes prepare an individual plate of fruit for each guest and pour about ¼ cup of warm sauce into individual ramekins. The sauce, a simple ganache, can be made in advance and simply warmed and brought to the table for dipping. You don't really need a special pot to enjoy a fondue party.

serves 6

1 recipe Pure Chocolate Sauce
(page 170)

Assorted fresh ripe fruit, washed, dried, and prepared:

Strawberries, with husks

Cherries, with stems

Pears, halved, cored, and thinly sliced lengthwise with skins on

Pineapple, peeled and cut in 1½-inch chunks

Apples, halved, cored, and thinly sliced lengthwise with skins on

Nectarines, halved, pits removed, and thinly sliced lengthwise with skins on

Orange segments, peeled

Shortbread cookies, biscotti, or sticks or squares of pound cake

Have ready the Pure Chocolate Sauce. Pour the warm sauce into a fondue pot or other small pot to a depth of 2 to 3 inches for dipping, or serve in individual ramekins as described above. Keep the pot of sauce warm at the table over a low flame or candle. Serve with individual long fondue forks or skewers for guests to dip their own dessert. Best consumed shortly after the fruit is cut.

VARIATION

For Caramel Fondue, prepare the recipe for Caramel Sauce (page 177). For 6 people, serve with crisp apples or crisp, ripe Bosc or Anjou pears (skin on), thinly sliced for dipping. Sprinkle the fruit with lemon juice to preserve color if cutting in advance.

black-and-white pavés

These pavés, or flat pieces of poured chocolate cut into squares or rectangles, are named after traditional French paving stones. With their contrasting layers of bittersweet and white chocolate, these elegant rectangles are so pretty they can hold their own on a tray of dipped and finished chocolates. The key is to be patient and wait for the exact right moment—when the chocolate just begins to thicken—to pour each layer.   makes about 96 pieces

bottom layer

17 ounces semisweet chocolate, finely chopped

1¼ cups heavy cream

3 tablespoons butter, room temperature

top layer

1 pound white chocolate, finely chopped

1 cup heavy cream

Have ready a 9-by-13-inch or quarter-sheet pan lined with parchment paper.

to prepare the bottom layer

Place the finely chopped dark chocolate in a bowl.

In a saucepan, heat the cream over medium-high heat just until it begins to boil. Remove from the heat and pour over the chocolate in the bowl. Stir until smooth with a rubber spatula and set aside to cool.

Gently stir the mixture every 10 minutes for about 40 minutes until it begins to mound on the surface but settles back into the mixture within 20 seconds. You do not want to incorporate any air, just start the setting process.

Before adding the butter, check that it is the same consistency as the ganache. If too hard, beat it to soften. Stir the softened butter into the chocolate until no traces remain.

Pour into the prepared pan. Spread evenly and smooth with an offset metal spatula.

to prepare the top layer

While the dark-chocolate ganache firms in the sheet pan for 1 to 2 hours, begin making the white-chocolate ganache.

Place the chopped white chocolate in a bowl.

In a saucepan, heat the cream over medium-high heat just until it begins to boil. Remove from the heat and pour over the white chocolate in the bowl. Stir until smooth with a rubber spatula.

Gently stir the mixture every 10 to 15 minutes for about 30 minutes in all, until it begins to mound on the surface but settles back within 20 seconds. You do not want to incorporate any air into the mixture, just start the setting process.

(continued)

Before pouring the white layer, check that the bottom is firm. It should look dull on top and hold a soft indent when pressed with a finger. Then pour the white chocolate over the dark layer. With an offset metal spatula spread evenly and smoothly.

Set aside to set up, uncovered, at least 8 to 12 hours at room temperature, but no longer than 24 hours.

To remove, run a thin knife around the pan to loosen the ganache. Turn out onto a parchment-lined board. Remove the parchment and invert again so that the white layer is on top.

Using a thin blade, cut the ganache into 8 strips lengthwise and 12 strips across the width, to make bite-size pieces.

Arrange on a parchment-lined pan and allow to set until firm to the touch, as long as 12 hours.

If desired, these black-and-white pavés may be dipped in chocolate (photograph page 208), following the instructions for tempered semisweet chocolate (page 193).

Undipped pavés: Can be stored tightly wrapped in the refrigerator for up to 5 days.

Dipped pavés: Stored between 60 and 68 degress, the pavés can be kept up to 2 weeks.

the gift of chocolate

*i*n France a beautiful box of chocolates is a common hostess gift. Fresh flowers can make the host jittery finding the right vase and a bottle of wine may imply that the host's wine selection is not up to par, but a box of chocolates is always in good taste. A friend in France admits to squirrelling away these chocolate gifts and saving them for her private enjoyment. The French know that personal pleasures demand focus.

Each box of chocolates that we sell is created as a complete sensory experience. We create a color palate for the holidays, custom ribbon is designed and ordered, thick vellum tissue paper is printed, and gold pads are trimmed. The candies must be packed perfectly, each piece in its own paper cup with the signature signs all lined up and symmetrical. When a fresh box of candies is opened, that first impression must fulfill on every level—sight, taste, and texture.

You needn't be as painstaking with your hand-made candies, but they do make a spectacular gift. Check out cake-decorating specialty shops and sources listed on page 227 for little paper and foil cups. You can also try crafts and stationery shops for tissue papers and pretty boxes. When packing the pieces, try to pack tightly to minimize movement and place a pad between the layers if possible. For serving chocolates at a party, silver trays are always a good choice. They underline the luxury of fine chocolates and contrast nicely with the dark brown color.

❖{ chocolate-stuffed figs }❖

Luscious stuffed figs speak to all the senses. They look like amber jewels, their texture feels meltingly soft in the mouth, the chocolate coating snaps when you take a bite, and the fragrance goes directly to the musky, sweet section of the brain. One glorious fig makes a complete dessert, or cut larger figs into quarters as part of a dessert tray. The very best, extra-fancy dried figs are in the market from October to March. Look for moist fruit with supple texture and full shape for stuffing. makes 24 to 36

1 cup heavy cream

8 ounces semisweet chocolate, finely chopped

24 to 36 dried Calimyrna figs, depending on size

1½ pounds semisweet chocolate, tempered (page 193) (optional)

Have ready a 9-by-13-inch or quarter-sheet pan lined with parchment.

In a saucepan, heat the cream over medium-high heat just until it begins to boil. Remove from the heat. Add the finely chopped chocolate. Stir until smooth with a rubber spatula. Pour the mixture into a bowl, cover with plastic wrap touching the top, and let set for 6 to 8 hours at room temperature.

Prepare figs for stuffing by gently rolling between your thumb and fingers to loosen the seeds and soften the flesh. Insert a wooden or metal skewer in the hole in the bottom of the fig and wiggle it to enlarge the hole slightly for stuffing.

When the ganache is set, gently stir with a rubber spatula a few times. Spoon into a pastry bag fitted with a small round ¼-inch tip (#803).

Hold each fig's stem gently between your index and middle fingers, using your thumb to support the plump fruit. Insert the tip of the pastry bag into the fig's bottom. Gently squeeze, stuffing until the fig is plump and full. Do not worry about leaks in the fig's skin. They can be fixed later.

Place filled figs on a parchment-lined pan and allow to set at room temperature for at least 2 hours. Using a sharp knife, scrape the excess filling from each fig's exterior. Stuffed figs can be stored in a sealed container in the refrigerator. Remove and return to room temperature for eating—or dipping, if desired.

To dip, follow the tempering and dipping instructions. Holding it by the stem, dip the bottom half of each fig in dark chocolate. Place the dipped fruit on a parchment-lined pan and let the chocolate set. With a pair of sharp scissors, snip off the very tip of each stem, which is too tough to be eaten, before serving.

(continued)

VARIATIONS

CHOCOLATE-STUFFED PRUNES

Soak about 48 dried pitted prunes in Cognac, Armagnac, or Calvados for 4 hours. Remove and drain on a rack until the surface is tacky, about 1 hour. Using a pastry bag fitted with a small round 1/4-inch tip (#803), fill each prune with the ganache and let set.

CHOCOLATE-STUFFED DATES

Soak 48 to 60 dates (preferably large, plump Medjool) in Cognac, Armagnac, or Calvados for 4 hours. Remove and drain on a rack until the surface is tacky, about 1 hour. Make a lengthwise slit and remove the pit. Using a #18 star tip, pipe ganache lengthwise into the centers. Then, using a circular motion, decorate the tops. Let set on a tray. Garnish the tops with finely chopped pistachios, if desired.

{ building blocks }

❧{ chocolate butter glaze }❧

Butter is what gives this gorgeous glaze its glossy finish and a silky feeling on the palate. I use it as the finishing touch on most of the classic European-style tortes. Butter-glazed cakes should always be stored at room temperature, since chilling dulls their shine.   makes enough for one 9-inch torte

4 ounces semisweet chocolate, finely chopped

1 stick (8 tablespoons) unsalted butter, room temperature

In a double boiler or bowl over simmering water, melt the chocolate. Remove the top of the boiler (or bowl) when the chocolate is nearly melted and continue stirring until smooth. Add the softened butter, slowly stirring with a rubber spatula until no visible traces of butter remain. (If the butter starts to liquefy, stop and let the chocolate cool slightly.) The glaze should be glossy and smooth with a temperature of 80–85°F. When stirred, it will hold a line on the surface for about 10 seconds before disappearing. If the glaze begins to set up, return briefly to the double boiler.

dark-chocolate ganache glaze

This traditional ganache gives cakes a lovely dark-chocolate velvet finish. The only techniques you need to remember are to start with a well-chilled cake and not to incorporate any air as you gently stir. A resilient ganache such as this one can be gently reheated and used again as a glaze, sauce, or filling. And it does not lose its sheen with refrigeration. You may halve the recipe for a single 9-inch round layer.

makes enough for 1 double-layer 9-inch round or quarter-sheet-pan layer cake

8 ounces semisweet chocolate, finely chopped

1 cup heavy cream

Place the chopped chocolate in a stainless-steel mixing bowl.

In a small saucepan heat the cream over medium-high heat until it begins to boil. Remove from the heat and pour over the chocolate. Let sit 1 minute and then start gently stirring with a rubber spatula from the center out, until smooth. Cool at room temperature about 30 minutes, uncovered, stirring occasionally, until the ganache thickens enough to ribbon off the end of the spatula when lifted. The ideal pouring temperature is 80–85°F.

If a recipe calls for a thin coating or masking prior to glazing, chill one quarter of the mixture for about 25 minutes. The purpose of masking is to seal in the filling and crumbs and give the glaze a smooth surface to stick to. This step is always optional but will give your cakes a professional high-gloss look. Use an offset spatula and a firm hand with constant pressure to apply a thin layer of ganache on all exposed surfaces before pouring the room-temperature glaze.

⊰} dark-chocolate truffle filling {⊱

When it comes to chocolate, you can't have too much of a good thing—in this case a smooth, rich filling for a totally chocolate layer cake. A thicker ganache like this is an excellent choice when you get the urge to decorate because it pipes so easily. See the Truffle Torte (page 96) and Chocolate Almond Macaroons (page 43) for inspiration.

makes enough to fill a 9-inch round 4-layer cake or a 9-by-13-inch 2-layer cake

1 cup heavy cream

9 ounces semisweet chocolate, finely chopped

In a saucepan heat the cream over medium-high heat just until it begins to boil. Remove from the heat and add the chocolate, stirring until the chocolate is smooth and melted. Pour the ganache into a small bowl, cover with plastic wrap touching the surface to prevent a skin from forming, and set aside. Let the ganache set up at room temperature for 8 to 12 hours or overnight.

To speed things up, you may let sit at room temperature, uncovered, about 4 hours. Gently fold with a spatula every 20 to 30 minutes until it thickens and becomes the consistency of soft butter.

⁂⊰ milk-chocolate hazelnut filling ⊱⁂

A rich, creamy milk-chocolate filling for any of your dark-chocolate layer cakes. I use it in the spectacular Triple Chocolate Pyramid (page 115) and Milk-Chocolate Hazelnut Roll (page 120). It would also be nice with your favorite yellow cake.

makes enough to fill a 9-inch round 4-layer cake or a 9-by-13-inch 2-layer cake

3 ounces semisweet chocolate

4 ounces milk chocolate

6 ounces gianduja (you may substitute 4 ounces additional milk chocolate and ¼ cup hazelnut paste—see Sources, page 227)

1 stick (8 tablespoons) unsalted butter, room temperature

In a double boiler or bowl melt the semisweet, milk, and gianduja chocolates over low heat. Remove when nearly melted and continue stirring until smooth. The mixture should be glossy and smooth. Set aside to cool to about 90°F. When ready, it should not feel warm to the touch.

In a mixer fitted with the paddle attachment, beat the butter on high speed 5 to 6 minutes until light in texture and pale in color, stopping several times to scrape down the sides of the bowl.

Pour the melted chocolate mixture all at once into the whipped butter. Continue beating 5 to 6 minutes on high speed until light and airy, stopping several times to scrape down the sides of the bowl. The finished mixture should be pale brown in color, with a smooth, glossy finish.

WHIPPED CREAMS

∗{ sweetened whipped cream }∗

Lightly whipped cream is a beautiful accompaniment to most chocolate desserts. I also love it as a light filling between cake layers. The trick with cream is to whip it cold and always err on the side of less rather than more time if you have any doubts about when to stop. Whipped cream can be made about 3 hours ahead. Store in the refrigerator.　　makes 1½ cups

1 cup heavy cream, chilled

2 tablespoons sugar

In a mixer with the whisk attachment, whip the cream starting at low speed and gradually increasing to medium as the cream thickens and creeps up the sides of the bowl. When traces of the whisk are visible in the cream, gradually sprinkle in the sugar, continuously whisking at high speed until soft peaks are formed. The entire procedure should take 2 to 3 minutes, and the peaks should fall back into the bowl when lifted.

⁖⸱{ white-chocolate whipped cream }⸱⁖

Chocolate helps the cream hold its shape longer without weeping, in addition to perfuming it with essence of cocoa butter. Such a tasty cream is lovely as a filling for cream puffs (page 166) or between layers of a cake, with perhaps a fruit layer for tartness. See the fabulous La Rêverie walnut cake (page 107) to inspire white-chocolate dreams.   makes 3 cups

6 ounces white chocolate, finely chopped

1½ cups heavy cream, chilled

In a double boiler or bowl melt the white chocolate over low heat. Remove when nearly melted and continue stirring until smooth. Let cool, returning to the double boiler briefly if it begins to set up.

Either by hand or using a mixer, lightly whip the cold cream until very soft peaks form and it just mounds in the bowl.

Working quickly, with a hand whisk add the lightly whipped cream all at once to the cooled melted chocolate. (If you reverse the order, chips will form.) Whisk until thoroughly combined, taking care not to overwhip and lose the smooth creamy consistency. Store in the refrigerator.

⁂{ cappuccino whipped cream }⁂

The combination of coffee and chocolate is one of the foolproof marriages of the dessert world. This coffee-spiked cream is luscious with any of the pure dark-chocolate desserts—the Espresso Torte (page 71) perhaps being the ultimate mocha pairing. Profiteroles of Cappuccino Whipped Cream topped with Deepest, Darkest Chocolate Sauce (page 172) are equally sublime.

makes 3½ cups

¼ cup plus 2 tablespoons sugar

3 tablespoons brewed espresso or 2 tablespoons water mixed with 2 tablespoons instant coffee (preferably freeze-dried)

2 cups heavy cream, chilled

Either by hand or using a mixer, whisk together the sugar and coffee until frothy. The sugar will begin to dissolve. Add the cream and whisk until thoroughly combined and soft peaks form. Take care not to overwhip the cream as it may begin to lose its creamy texture. Store in the refrigerator.

⁂⦃ caramel whipped cream ⦄⁂

This tan-colored cream is wonderful between the layers of a dark-chocolate cake or served alongside any of the chilled desserts. Caramel is always an excellent complementary flavor to toasted nuts, and it goes especially well with the Chocolate Caramel Nut Tart (page 85).   makes 3½ cups

½ cup Caramel Sauce (page 177), chilled

2 cups heavy cream, chilled

In a bowl combine the Caramel Sauce and 1 cup of the cream. Stir well to dissolve the caramel. Then add the remaining cream, stirring until smooth. Either by hand or using a mixer, lightly whip the cream until it just mounds in the bowl. Take care not to overwhip the cream and lose its creamy texture. Place in the refrigerator until ready to use.

TART CRUSTS

⁍ chocolate wafer tart crust ⁌

This crisp chocolate cookie crust can be used for just about any tart—the choice is yours. I am partial to a chocolate crust with nuts and caramel, but you may consider any combination that works with a crisp chocolate cookie: Princess Pudding (page 140), white-chocolate ganache topped with raspberries, a smooth layer of espresso-infused mousse, or the Pure Chocolate Tart filling (page 79). The full recipe makes two crusts; cut the dough quantity in half for one shell or a dozen small tarts.

makes enough for two 9-inch round tart shells or twenty-four 3-inch round tart shells (Halve the recipe for one 9-inch tart shell.)

1 recipe Chocolate Wafers dough (page 39)

Wrap the dough for the Chocolate Wafers well in plastic and chill until firm, about 4 hours, or overnight.

to roll out the dough

Lightly butter one 9-inch round fluted tart pan or twelve 3-inch round fluted tart pans with removable bottoms.

For one tart shell, remove the dough from the refrigerator and cut in half. Rewrap and store the second portion in the refrigerator or freezer for another tart. Let the remaining dough warm on the counter for about 20 minutes, until pliable but still cool to the touch.

On a lightly floured board gently knead the dough a few times. Pat into a ball, then with the palms of your hands flatten into a 5-inch round disk. With a floured rolling pin, begin rolling from the center out,

lifting and turning until an 11½-inch circle, about ⅛ inch thick, is formed. Keep dusting the board and pin with all-purpose flour as needed.

Gently lift and roll the dough onto the rolling pin, brushing off any excess flour with a pastry brush. Place the dough in the buttered tart pan and unroll, taking care not to roll the pin along the top edge of the pan.

Press the dough evenly over the bottom and around the edges of the pan, keeping the sides even and thick. (Cracks can be repaired by lightly moistening the broken edges with a few drops of water and patching with small scraps of dough.) Using a sharp paring knife, trim excess dough along the edges. Pierce the bottom with the tines of a fork and place in the refrigerator. Chill for at least 30 minutes or until firm.

to bake an empty tart shell

Position a rack in the middle of the oven and preheat the oven to 350°F.

Place the chilled tart shell on a baking sheet. Bake for 20 to 25 minutes, until the top is blistered and dry. The shell should feel firm to the touch. It will crisp as it cools.

VARIATION

For 3-inch round individual tarts, roll the dough out into a rectangle, about 9 by 12 inches. Cut out circles with a 4-inch round cookie cutter. Transfer the circles of dough to the buttered tart pans, pressing into the bottom and sides following the same procedure as for a larger tart. Bake small tarts at 350°F for 18 to 20 minutes. Dough scraps may be gathered, returned to the refrigerator to chill, and rerolled.

{ a tart's temperature }

the key to a fabulous tender tart crust is temperature. When very cold dough goes into a hot oven, the same process occurs that we see so dramatically with puff pastry—the heat in the oven causes the cold butter to expand, forming the air bubbles that create a light pastry. If the dough is too warm before baking, the butter leaks out in the oven, resulting in a greasy pan and dense, tough crust. I keep my freezer stocked with lined tart pans ready for the oven.

❋{ sugar tart crust }❋

This easy-to-handle French tart dough is as simple as it is superb. If you follow the instructions step by step, you'll have a wonderful crumbly, slightly sweet cookie dough that won't shrink or puff when baked, eliminating the need for pie weights. Low-gluten cake flour makes all the difference—it stays short and crisp, without tightening in the oven. The only trick you need to know for rolling any tart dough is to handle it lightly and return it to the refrigerator if it becomes too soft to handle.

makes enough for one 9-inch round tart shell or twelve 3-inch round tart shells

¾ stick (6 tablespoons) unsalted butter, room temperature

¼ cup sugar

1 large egg yolk

1 cup cake flour

all-purpose flour for dusting

In a mixer fitted with the paddle attachment, cream together the butter and sugar on medium-high speed, about 2 minutes. Scrape down the sides of the bowl.

Add the egg yolk. Continue mixing on medium-high speed for 1 to 2 minutes, until pale yellow in color and completely smooth. Scrape down the sides of the bowl.

Add the cake flour. Mix on low speed just until blended, being careful not to over-mix. Transfer to a sheet of plastic wrap and gently pat into a ball. Wrap well and chill for at least 2 hours or overnight.

to roll out the dough

Lightly butter a 9-inch round tart pan or twelve 3-inch round tart pans with removable bottoms.

Remove the chilled dough from the refrigerator. Let the dough warm on the counter for about 20 minutes, until pliable but still cool to the touch.

On a lightly floured board gently knead the dough a few times. Pat into a ball, then with the palms of your hands flatten into a 5-inch round disk. With a floured rolling pin, begin rolling from the center out, lifting and turning until an 11½-inch circle, about ⅛ inch thick, is formed. Keep dusting the board and pin with all-purpose flour as needed.

Gently lift and roll the dough onto the rolling pin, brushing off any excess flour with a pastry brush. Place the dough in the buttered tart pan and unroll, taking care not to roll the pin along the top edge of the pan.

Press the dough into the bottom and around the edges of the pan, keeping the sides even and thick. (Cracks can be repaired by lightly moistening the broken edges with a few drops of water and patching with small scraps of dough.) Using a sharp paring knife, trim excess dough along the edges. Pierce the bottom with the tines of a fork and place in the refrigerator. Chill for at least 30 minutes or until firm.

to bake an empty tart shell

Position a rack in the middle of the oven and preheat the oven to 350°F.

Place the chilled tart shell on a baking sheet. Bake for 20 to 25 minutes, until the top is blistered and dry. The shell should feel firm to the touch. It will crisp as it cools.

VARIATION

For 3-inch round individual tarts, roll the dough out into a rectangle, about 9 by 12 inches. With a 4-inch round cookie cutter cut out circles. Transfer the circles of dough to the buttered tart pans, pressing into the bottom and sides following the same procedure as for a larger tart. Bake small tarts at 350°F for 18 to 20 minutes. Dough scraps may be gathered, returned to the refrigerator to chill, and rerolled.

❧ walnut tart crust ❧

A rich nut crust like this is the easiest for the beginning baker since it is pressed into the pan rather than rolled. Similar to a linzer torte crust, it is delicious baked and filled with a good raspberry jam and topped with a layer of Dark-Chocolate Truffle Filling (page 216). In the autumn I fill a prebaked nut shell with fresh cranberries—cooked with sugar just long enough to pop. And for Thanksgiving I make this crust with pecans to hold a traditional pumpkin filling.

makes one 9-inch tart crust

2⅓ cups walnuts or pecans

½ cup slivered blanched almonds

3 tablespoons sugar

¾ stick (6 tablespoons) unsalted butter, room temperature

1 tablespoon pure vanilla extract

Lightly butter a 9-inch round fluted tart pan with a removable bottom.

Pulse the walnuts in a food processor until finely ground. Remove and set aside. Add the almonds and the sugar. Pulse, scraping down the bowl several times, until ground into a powder.

In a mixer fitted with the paddle attachment, cream the butter on medium-high speed until fluffy, about 2 minutes. Add the vanilla and blend thoroughly. Add the nut mixture and mix on low speed until the dough begins to hold together.

Press the dough evenly into the bottom and sides of the tart pan. Cover with plastic wrap and refrigerate 1 hour or freeze until firm, about ½ hour.

to bake an empty tart shell

Position a rack in the middle of the oven and preheat the oven to 350°F.

Unwrap the shell and place on a baking sheet. Prick all over with the tines of a fork. Bake for 10 to 13 minutes, until the crust feels dry and looks puffy. Remove from the oven and gently press the bottom down with the back of a wooden spoon. Return to the oven for 8 to 12 minutes, or until lightly golden brown. Transfer to rack and cool completely.

sources

Bridge Kitchenware

214 East 52nd Street
New York, NY 10022
800–274–3435
*This New York store has professional-quality
pastry and cooking equipment, including
cardboard cake rounds, parchment paper,
cake pans, and tart rings.*

King Arthur's Flour Company
Baker's Catalogue

P.O. Box 876
Norwich, VT 05055
800–827–6836
kingarthurflour.com
*A great source for equipment and ingredients
for the home baker, including cake flour,
almond flour, decorative sugars, hazelnut
paste, madeleine pans, dipping forks, and
candy papers*

Surfas Restaurant Supply

8825 National Boulevard
Culver City, CA 90232
surfasonline.com
310–559–4770
*This warehouse-style store, open to the public,
stocks Valrhona and Callebaut in bulk,
including my favorite semisweet with 56 percent cacao and gianduja. Also: cake boxes,
boards, parchment paper cones, and baking
equipment*

Sur La Table

800–243–0852
surlatable.com
*This national chain based in Seattle carries
all of the equipment called for in the recipes,
including professional flare-sided round cake
pans for the tortes. Catalog and web sales*

Williams-Sonoma

800–541–2233
williams-sonoma.com
*The national cookware chain has an extensive
selection of bakeware as well as chocolates for
baking.*

manufacturers

*Chocolate makers' websites are good sources
for finding chocolate.*

Callebaut

800–774–9131
ecallebaut.com

El Rey

800–EL–REY–99
elreychocolate.com

Guittard

800–468–2462
eguittard.com

Scharffen Berger

510–981–4050
scharffenberger.com

Valrhona

310–277–0401
valrhona.com

INDEX

Page number in *italics* refer to illustrations.

Coconut:
  Cream White-Chocolate Bars, 44–46, *45*
  Tropicale Roll, 126–28, *127*
  White-Chocolate Ice Cream, 149
Coffee, 13, 20
  Cappuccino Cream Cake, 110–11
  Cappuccino Whipped Cream, 220
  Chocolate Espresso Sauce, 171
  Chocolate Espresso Torte, 71–72
  Espresso Bites, 200–201
  Milk-Chocolate Mocha Tart, *82*, 83
  Mocha Ricotta Torte, 105–6
  White-Chocolate Espresso Semifreddo,
    161–62
Confectioners' sugar, 18
Cookies, 41
  Chocolate Almond Macaroons, 43
  Chocolate Madeleines, 48–49
  Chocolate Meringues, 37
  Chocolate Sablés, 40–41
  Chocolate Tuile Cups, 47
  Chocolate Wafers, *38*, 39
  Pure Chocolate Chunk, 42
  White-Chocolate Coconut Cream Bars,
    44–46, *45*
  See also Brownies
Cranberry Nut Tart variation, 78
Cream, 18
  Torte, Chilled Almond, 156–57
  See also Ice Cream; Whipped cream
Creaming butter and sugar, 41, 53
Cream Puffs (Profiteroles), Chocolate, 166,
  167
Crème Anglaise, 173
  Belgian Chocolate Cheesecake, 130–32, *131*
  Chocolate, 173
  Chocolate Cabernet Torte, 73–74, *75*
Crème Brûlée, Chocolate, 137–39, *138*
Crème fraîche:
  Dylan's Birthday Cake, 95
  L'Etoile, 112–14, *113*
Crust, Tart:
  Chocolate Wafer, 222–23
  Sugar, 224–25
  temperature of, 223
  Walnut, 226

Crystal sugars, 18
Cups, Chocolate Tuile, 47
Curls, chocolate, how to make, 14–15, *15*
Custard:
  Chocolate Crème Brûlée, 137–39, *138*
  Chocolate Pots de Crème, 142–43
  Crème Anglaise, 173
  Triple-Chocolate Parfait, 163–65, *164*

d

Dark chocolate, 11
  melting and tempering, 16, 190
Date, Chocolate-stuffed, 212
Decorating:
  with candied flowers, 114
  dipped chocolates, 193
  white chocolate writing, 104, *104*
Decorative sugars, 18
Dipped chocolates, 190, 193, 201
Dried fruits, 20
  See also Fruit
Dylan's Birthday Cake, 95

e

Egg(s), 18
  adding to melted chocolate, 13
  whites, whipping, 63
  yolks, beating sugar with, 53
Equipment, 21–27
  sources for, 227
Espresso, 13, 20
  Bites, 200–201
  Cappuccino Cream Cake, 110–11
  Cappuccino Whipped Cream, 220
  Chocolate Sauce, 171
  Chocolate Torte, 71–72
  Mocha Ricotta Torte, 105–6
  White Chocolate Semifreddo, 161–62
L'Etoile, 112–14, *113*

f

Fat bloom, 14
Figs, Chocolate-stuffed, 210–12, *211*